D1740918

Navy Bites:

the Strange, the Great, and the Tragic of the Royal Navy

Volume I

by

AJ Noon

This book is dedicated to the amazing people who take the time to attend museums and engage with the docents - it's easy to read information panels and listen to audio guides, but asking questions brings your visit to life (and makes our life more interesting – we are not there just for health and safety!).

Publishing Information

1st Published July 2023

Version 1.2a

ISBN: 978-1-8384332-5-3

www.redvarkpublishing.co.uk

redvarkpub@gmail.com *@redvarkpub*

A ridiculous amount of thanks (as always) to KSL for her hard work

Table of Contents

24th April 1546 – The Isle of Wight Leads to the Royal Navy 7

26th November 1703 – A Cruel Wind 12

1747 - Hannah Snell Joins the Royal Marines 13

10th March 1777 – Fire and Tar 16

29th August 1782 – George Goes Down 19

24th July 1797 – Cold Steel 23

19th October 1798 – The Impregnable Fails 26

3rd February 1804 – An Extreme Row 28

3rd June 1805 – A Stone Frigate Falls 30

21st October 1805 – Confiding in Your Expectations 33

16th May 1811 – A Presidential Affair 35

1812 Who needs Ikea? 38

22nd September 1835 – A Ship of Stone 39

3rd April 1845 – A Naval Tug of War 41

8th June 1897 – False Information 43

1899 – Lord Nelson at the Siege of Mafeking 45

30th October 1899 – Guns on the Run 46

26th December 1915 – Heading Inland 49

21st May 1915 – Hiding a Submarine 53

7th June 1917 – Two Become One 56

31st January 1918 – A Bad Practice 60

21st June 1919 – Any Old Steel 65

25th August 1939 – A Naval Nuisance 68

16th February 1940 – Pirates in Norway 69

9th December 1942 – One Becomes Two 75

2nd September 1942 – Duties for Apes 76

16th May 1943 – The Navy Inspires a Bounce 78

1943 – If It Floats – Use It 81

1959 – Nuclear London 83

July 31st 1970 – An Odd Burial 85

May 30th 1982 – HMS Invincible... Still Afloat 87

24th September 1993 – The Black Flag of Monmouth 90

Index 100

Naval Children's Charity

Supporting children whose parents serve or have served in the Royal Navy.

The Naval Children's Charity are delighted to be supported by the sales of this book and we do hope that you really enjoy reading it.

Introduction

The Royal Navy was formed over four-hundred-and-seventy years ago, and like all organisations with a long history, it has had successes, failures, and suffered the whimsies of fate. Some of the events I have covered here are acts of bravery by men ordered to fight for their country, whether they wanted to or not, and others are tragic occurrences such as the loss of a ship. There are men and ships whose names you will be familiar with, some you will meet several times, and others you may have never heard of.

At the time of writing this book, I work for the National Museum of the Royal Navy and am in the privileged position of having to talk about the Royal Navy every day to the public. Every so often someone will mention something intriguing that I am unaware of – and it is these snippets that led to this book.

When a well-travelled visitor asks me about ships made from two different ones, flat-pack ships, the Royal Navy enlisting a dog (and not as a mascot), or women in the Royal Marines, I must dig further to find an answer (and the truth of the matter) for them should they return or if I am asked about it again.

Sometimes the details have been lost over time, and for others they are so well documented there is almost too much information. From all the pieces I have learnt and researched over the years, this volume contains some of those that made an impression on me – for good or bad.

The incidents in this book are organised by date of occurrence, and for events that spanned many months or years I have picked a key date in that span.

AJ Noon

We are a small independent publisher, and reviews mean everything to us. The world of books is ruled by algorithms and the visibility of this book, and our others, relies on you the reader leaving a review. You have given us your precious time to read this book, which we already greatly appreciate, but if we could ask you to leave an honest review on the review site of your choice (Amazon, LibraryThing, Book Riot, Booklist, LoveReading, Goodreads, etc), then you have our gratitude.

Your reviews also help shape our future books as we get a better idea of what our readers like and want more of.

Redvark Publishing Limited

Before I start, I need to highlight something important - the collective noun for historians is an *'argumentation'*. If you are taking history seriously, you cannot just read one source, you have to read many sources from the period and then attempt to draw conclusions. You have to take into account the mindset of the time, the bias of each source, and which political/religious message is being portrayed at the time it was written. As you get closer in time to the present day, these are somewhat easier to both research and interpret, but the further back you go then the more biased the sources tend to become.

Whilst writing this book I have tried to consider the sources, the bias, and what the authors at the time may have been trying to convey. Though I focus on stories of the Royal Navy, I am acutely aware that I need to give a balanced telling of events.

I was brought up on the war films of old, *'The Dam Busters'*, *'Sink the Bismarck'*[1], *'The Battle of the River Plate'*, *'The Longest Day'*, and so on. These films were as much propaganda as storytelling, and though they may be a good introduction to these events, they also highlight the need for our future historians – hopefully in my case my grandchildren – to be aware of critical thinking.

This applies in all walks of life – we know (or we should know) which political leaning each newspaper and news website has, as well as the bias of the various streaming sources on YouTube or similar channels. My last entry in this book, about the Falklands, highlights this perfectly – if you watch one video on the internet about an event, the algorithms that promulgate recommended content will show you videos that match the one you have watched, not ones that give you an alternative or differing view (or even a factually correct article).

We have a responsibility to our future generations to ensure they are aware of critical thinking, the perfidiousness of computer algorithms, and the importance of primary sources, not just published works. With more sources being digitised, access to them is becoming easier and cheaper – but we still have to ensure that researchers take into consideration any subtext of the source.

As with *'The Trafalgar Times'*, which I publish and edit, I hope readers use this book as a starting point to do their own reading and research, and not as the endpoint. The events here cover nearly five-hundred years – spanning multiple rulers, multiple religions, and multiple wars – and I want the stories to inspire you to find out more and delve-deeper.

---

[1] *'Sink the Bismarck'* is a great example of propaganda – though the ship was inevitably doomed, the Germans opened the seacocks to scuttle her before the incoming fire did the job. It is also important to note that though 1,413 men were killed on *HMS Hood* when she was sunk, when *Bismarck* went down over 2,000 men lost their lives.

24th April 1546 – The Isle of Wight Leads to the Royal Navy

In 1545, Henry VIII was on the throne, and though England had ships and sailors, she did not have a standing navy[2]. When he came to rule on the 22nd of April 1509, aged just 17, he inherited seven – yes seven – warships from his father, Henry VII.

Henry VII had started to increase the number of ships he could call on, and spent money on improving the facilities of the dockyards, but it was his son that continued this work in earnest. By 1513, Henry VIII's navy had twenty-three ships, including the *Mary Rose*, and the following year construction was finished on the *Henry Grace à Dieu*, also known as the *'Great Harry'* (*below*). This was the largest warship in the world at the time[3], carrying around 700 sailors and soldiers, and was the first English ship to feature two gun-decks.

---

[2] There were *'King's Ships'*, but these were called into action when needed, rather than being a patrolling force as we would know now.

[3] She was around 165-feet long, weighed around 1,000 tons when supplied, and carried 43 main guns (as well as an array of swivel guns of smaller sizes).

If we wind the clock back to pre-1066, England and France were neighbours who tolerated each other but didn't really have any fights – both were a collection of kingdoms and duchies that had been pre-occupied with internal power-struggles and the Vikings rather than the countries as we recognise them now[4]. Then, in 1066, after the death of his distant cousin Edward the Confessor, along comes the Duke of Normandy claiming he had been promised the throne of England. Unfortunately, he also brought to England a large fleet carrying an equally large army, and after defeating Harold Godwinson at the Battle of Hastings he took the throne, becoming William I of England, more commonly known as William the Conqueror[5].

You might think that is enough to start a beef[6] between England and France, but it was the centuries that followed that plunged relationships into more and more turmoil. The English and French nobility inter-married, leading to claims and counterclaims on various territories and thrones in both countries (not to mention the royal houses of other European countries). When you throw religion into the mix as well, especially Protestant and Catholic beliefs, then you can clearly see why there have been over twenty wars between the two countries since 1066.

One of the major ones was the so-called Italian Wars[7], between 1494 and 1559. Covering sixty-five years, they were a long series of battles during which England switched sides twice. Initially on the side of the Italian states, the Holy Roman Empire, and the Spanish, they switched to supporting France in 1526. A further change of heart meant that in 1542 they went back to their old allies, much to the chagrin of Francis I of France[8].

---

[4] The Kingdom of England was founded in 927 under King Æthelstan. The history of France is far more convoluted and there are arguments for either Clovis I as King of the Franks from 509, or the Kingdom of France forming in 987 under Hugh Capet, also known as King of the Franks. Luckily this book is about the Royal Navy, so I don't have to try to explain their history!

[5] Also known as William the Bastard as he was illegitimate son of Robert the Magnificent.

[6] Okay, a small pun here - the French nickname for the English became '*les rosbifs*', but this didn't enter the language until the 1700's. There was a song by Richard Loveridge, '*Our Fathers Of Old Were Robust, Stout, And Strong*' where the chorus line is '*O, the Roast Beef of old England*'. Add to this the French noting the English habit of ensuring the soldiers in the English-held settlements in France had roast beef to eat to make them feel less homesick, whereas they tended to boil meat. It is around the mid 1770's that this term for the English is first recorded as being used as an insult.

[7] Also known as the Habsburg-Valois Wars.

[8] Francis I was born in 1494 and ruled from 1515 to 1547. It was he who met Henry VIII at the '*Field of the Cloth of Gold*' in 1520, the meeting in France between the two kings that is renowned for the ridiculous display of wealth from both sides as they tried to impress each other.

Francis, deciding he needed to put England in her place, amassed a huge fleet in 1545 of some two-hundred ships which were carrying at least 30,000 soldiers. At this time, the English held Boulogne, an important port for both military and trade, which was being constantly re-supplied from the southern English ports, especially Portsmouth – making Portsmouth and her docks a prime target for France[9].

On July 18th, the French fleet reached the anchorage point of St. Helen's Roads, off the eastern tip of the Isle of Wight near Bembridge. Knowing they were coming, Henry had managed to supplement his ships, raising a fleet of some one-hundred vessels, including carracks like the *Mary Rose* and much smaller vessels, but though reinforced he was still outnumbered and was struggling with crewing and provisioning the ships.

In his favour were the defences on the coast he had ordered built, including Southsea Castle, Hirst Castle, and Calshot Castle. These fortifications were built from 1539 when Henry issued a *'device'* (an order). They were mostly finished by the time the French arrived, making a direct attack on Portsmouth harbour a troublesome prospect.

There was a minor engagement between the two fleets on the 18th in the Solent, but the French withdrew back behind the Isle of Wight with no real damage to either side. On the morning of the 19th, the winds were so low that the English could not sail, yet tucked in amongst the French fleet were many galleys, all of which carried oars so they could manoeuvre. The galleys, being smaller and nimbler than the larger carracks[10], took pot-shots at the English whilst the return fire generally went over the French heads, but as the morning progressed the wind picked up.

The larger British ships hoisted their sails, setting out towards the French, and it is then that disaster struck – the loss of the *Mary Rose*. As she went down, Henry VIII could only watch in horror from his vantage point at Southsea Castle.

The French claimed they hit her, her Captain Sir George Carew blamed his inexperienced crew as the ship was handling badly (he shouted as much to the captain of a nearby ship[11]), and some believe a gust of wind caused her to heel over. Whatever the cause, the outcome was inevitable; as she heeled, water

---

[9] French troops had previously raided Portsmouth in 1338, 1369, 1377, and 1380.

[10] Carracks were ships with three or more masts, capable of ocean travel, such as the *Mary Rose*.

[11] He is said to have shouted *"I have the sort of knaves I cannot rule"* to his uncle Gawen Carew on a neighbouring ship before the accident.

flooded in through her open gunports on the starboard side[12], causing the ship to founder. Some seven-hundred souls were lost onboard, and though the English had lost one of their larger ships, the French ended up withdrawing again to the Isle of Wight.

Most people know the tale of the *Mary Rose*, and how she was raised from the seabed in 1982. Most also know of the museum in Portsmouth where the wreck is displayed, along with some 19,000 objects that were retrieved at the same time. However, many people aren't aware of what the French did next in 1545.

With such a large fleet, and all those soldiers, the logical step was to invade the Isle of Wight. If you can't get to Portsmouth, you can make a base and re-supply from the island, especially if you can capture the fortifications there. It also puts you in a strong position to blockade shipping trying to leave the Solent, whether from Portsmouth or Southampton. So began the invasion of the Isle of Wight.

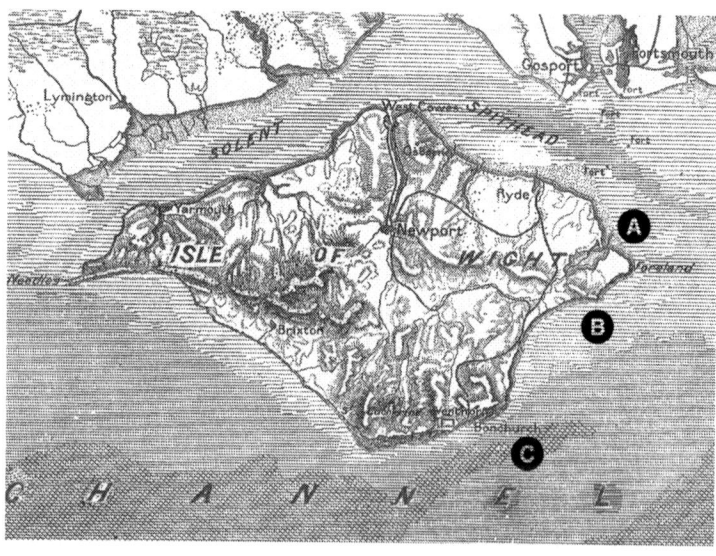

The French landed several thousand men at three different locations: St. Helens, Ⓐ Sandown, Ⓑ and Bonchurch Ⓒ, with the plan for them to push inland and then join up. There was a small fort at St. Helens, which fell quickly to the overwhelming numbers, and at Bonchurch the defenders were overpowered at the second

---

[12] The Portuguese standardised the use of gunports in around 1490 (though they had been used ad hoc for several decades before this). Initially they were just holes cut into the sides of ships, then lids started being added so they could be sealed in rough weather (and for protection from incoming fire). In 1643 it was recorded that England, France, and Holland used lids that were hinged at the top, whereas the Spanish used lids that were hinged at the side.

attempt, with both sides taking heavy losses. The local militia[13] were well trained, especially with the bow, and took the high ground to punish the French invaders. One of the defenders, Captain Robert Fyssher, was of portly stature and when the French were advancing on his position allegedly cried out for a horse, offering one-hundred pounds to anyone who could bring him one. No-one did, and he was never seen again, presumably captured by the French. Could he be the man who inspired Shakespeare's *'A horse, my kingdom for a horse!'* in Richard III?[14]

The third incursion, at Sandown, failed when the militia rushed the invaders before they could fortify their positions, fighting them on the beaches and forcing them back to their ships. Eventually, the other two invading forces followed suit and returned to their ships. The invasion of the Isle of Wight was over.

If the French had landed more troops, they would have quickly overwhelmed the defenders – the total population of the island at the time was only around 9,000 – but with the threat of the British fleet so close they were reluctant to take that measure.

Another small force landed a few days later in the search for fresh water, but they were repelled, and the French gave up on the whole idea, retreating across the English Channel, though they did stop and burn Seaford[15] before being forced back by the local militia (again).

The English fleet had little to do with this withdrawal, it was weather conditions, sickness, and low provisions amongst the French that contributed greatly, but it spurred Henry into further action with the plans for his fleet. Prior to 1546, one of the key positions was *'Keeper of the King's Ports and Galleys'* - later known as the *'Clerk of the King's Ships'*. Alongside this position, from 1514, was *'Keeper of the Storehouses'*, and in 1522 the position of *'Clerk Comptroller'* was added. By 1545, *'Master of Naval Ordnance'*, *'Treasurer of Marine Causes'*, *'Lieutenant of the Admiralty'*, and *'Surveyor and Rigger of the Navy'* were also created, and they formed a council called the *'King's Majesty Council of his Marine'*.

On the 24th of April 1546, aggrieved by the problems the British ships had suffered during the previous year, Henry issued patents officially creating the *'Navy Board'*. This provided a clear structure for the navy – for the construction and maintenance

---

[13] The militia system of England was originally an Anglo-Saxon concept, and by 1511 *'commissioners of array'* could raise common men into a temporary army and were also responsible for ensuring they were well-equipped. In 1519, Italian ambassadors believed that around 150,000 men across the country could be called into the militia – which does lead to the question of why the Italians wanted to know this information...

[14] *Richard III* was written between 1592 and 1594.

[15] Seaford is in East Sussex, between Brighton and Eastbourne.

of ships, for the supplies they required, and for the crews to man them. Also created was the *'Admiralty and Marine Affairs Office'*, led by the Lord High Admiral, and which dictated where the fleets should go and how they should operate.

It is this date, the 24th of April 1564, that is recognised as the date the Royal Navy was formed.

26th November 1703[16] – A Cruel Wind

Sailing ships rely on the wind, but it can be a double-edged sword: not enough and your ships are becalmed, too much and your ships are at risk of sinking. For the older reader, you may remember the so-called Great Storm of 1987, when on the night of the 15th of October, a storm-front rolled in over Southern England. In the early hours of the 16th, England was subjected to regular gusts of up to 70mph[17], with peak gusts of up to 120mph. Once the storm had passed, eighteen people had lost their lives and an estimated fifteen-million trees had been downed in England. The loss of life was low for a storm of such magnitude, but if we go back two-hundred-and-eighty-four years we find a much more damaging storm.

This one arrived on the evening of the 24th of November 1703 and blew through England for a week. The Eddystone lighthouse, off Cornwall, was swept away and across London the chimney stacks on the great buildings were being blown down. It even forced Queen Anne to take shelter in the cellars of St. James' Palace. There are no reliable numbers for those killed by the storm, but the losses to both merchant and naval vessels were huge. Thirty ships in a large convoy that took shelter at Milford Haven, Wales, were sunk, along with countless other merchant ships and fishing vessels.

A naval convoy heading back to England was blown onto the Goodwin Sands, off the coast of Kent, resulting in the loss of four third-rates: *HMS Restoration, HMS Stirling Castle*[18], *HMS Mary* and *HMS Northumberland*. The second-rate, *HMS Vanguard*[19], was wrecked at Chatham, and *HMS Association* had a miraculous

---

[16] Using the Julian calendar, which England did at the time. Under the Gregorian calendar this would be the 7th of December.

[17] Brittany and Normandy, France, recorded gusts of over 130 mph.

[18] There has been extensive diving and research on the wreck of Stirling Castle, and there is a very good virtual tour of the wreck at: www.cloudtour.tv/stirling.

[19] She was later re-floated and repaired.

escape - she was anchored off Harwich, Essex, when the storm ripped her from her moorings. In danger of being overwhelmed, the sailors cut away her rigging and she was blown all the way to Gothenburg, Sweden!

Other Royal Navy ships lost include *HMS Newcastle*, *HMS Reserve*, *HMS Vesuvius*, *HMS Litchfield Prize*, *HMS Resolution*, *HMS Eagle*, *HMS York*, and *HMS Mortar-Bomb*. That storm cost the Royal Navy one second-rate, four third-rates, four fourth-rates, three fifth-rates, and a sixth-rate, and the estimates to the number of men (both sailors and soldiers) varies from eight-thousand up to ten-thousand or more. The higher numbers equate to around a third of the Royal Navy strength at the time.

1747 - Hannah Snell Joins the Royal Marines

In October 1990, the Royal Navy took on a major upgrade and allowed women to officially serve onboard ships at sea. Twenty women from the Women's Royal Navy Service – nicknamed the '*Wrens*'[20] – joined *HMS Brilliant*, which was then deployed in the Persian Gulf during the First Gulf War (2nd August 1990 to 28th February 1991).

The Wrens were formed on the 29th of November 1917, to help supplement the shortfall in staffing caused by the losses during World War I[21]. They mainly took on clerical roles but that soon spread to include other shore-based jobs[22], and eventually included roles such as aircraft-handlers[23].

Once the war ended in 1918, the Admiralty didn't have a requirement for women in the service and the Wrens were disbanded the following year. In 1937, with clouds gathering over Europe once more, Dame Katharine Furse approached the Admiralty to suggest that the Wrens would be needed again, and they were officially re-formed on the 22nd of November 1938. After the war, the Wrens were

---

[20] Also '*Jennies*', short for '*Jenny Wren*', after the bird.

[21] There were already women helping in some shore-based tasks at this point, but a proper organisation and structure was needed for them.

[22] Not just in the UK either, they were also at bases in places such as Gibraltar and Malta.

[23] Despite being shore-based, one Wren was killed by enemy action during World War I. Josephine Carr was onboard *RMS Leinster* travelling from Dun Laoghaire to Holyhead to take up her first position. The ship was torpedoed on October the 10th, 1918, by *UB-123*, resulting in the loss of over 500 lives. Carr had joined the Wrens two weeks prior to the sinking, and the war ended only four weeks later.

retained, but it took until 1990 for them to be allowed to serve on ships. The Women's Royal Navy Service was fully integrated into the Royal Navy in 1993.

If we wind the clock back, we can find numerous examples of women on Royal Naval ships in a variety of roles prior to the Twentieth Century. In the Age of Sail, some Warrant Officers[24] would take their wives (and often children) onboard. In times of battle, the women would help in the surgeon's cockpit or with the handling of the gunpowder charges around the ship. At the Battle of Trafalgar in 1805, there are claims for at least three women onboard *HMS Victory*[25] during the battle, and on *HMS Defiance*[26] and *HMS Tonnant*.

Though they helped during the battle, they weren't officially serving[27], and we need to go a little further back to find what is probably the best example of a woman serving in the Royal Navy, albeit disguised as a man.

Hannah Snell was born in Worcester in 1723 into a relatively well-off family (she and her siblings received an education). After her parents died, she moved to London, and this is where the story gets a bit convoluted.

We know she moved in with her sister and brother-in-law, and according to the more

---

[24] At this time, Warrant Officers were skilled individuals who had a Warrant signed by the Admiralty allowing them to serve on board. They include the master, the bosun, the carpenter, the gunner, the sailmaker, the surgeon, and the cook.

[25] Mary Buick, Sarah Pitt, and Mary Sperring.

[26] Jane Townshend.

[27] Only men were listed in the muster books.

elaborate accounts she married a Dutch sailor in 1744. She fell pregnant, but instead of a happy family her husband left her, and her child died at a young age. Left in debt by her feckless husband, and with no ties to anyone or anything, she set out to find the man who had abandoned her – and hopefully recover the money. Knowing that as a woman she would not get very far, she talked her brother-in-law into lending her one of his suits and disguised herself as a man, taking the name of her brother-in-law, James Gray.

There is no evidence of this first marriage, and though there is a biography from the time it was written with the aid of a writer so is probably heavily embellished to make it more saleable. The first version of her story was 46 pages long, the second version extended to 187 pages, so there were definitely some additions to her story!

Snell (*right*) definitely signed up for the army as James Grey, joining the 6th Regiment of Foot, but after receiving 500 lashes she deserted, fleeing to Portsmouth. Here she joined the Royal Marines, where she served two years with them. She fought at Pondicherry in India and then Devicottail, where she received multiple injuries to her legs and groin. To avoid her ruse being uncovered, she took the medical assistance from a local rather than the navy surgeon (according to the biography - she may just have managed to conceal her private parts from the naval surgeon).

When the unit returned to England in 1750, the 'lads' went out drinking, and at one point during the night James Gray stood up and revealed themselves as actually being a woman.

Her account was written up as '*The Female Soldier*', and she reclaimed her real name. She went on to perform in the theatre, dressing up in her uniform and performing the drill-routines she had been taught, as well as singing popular songs. She re-married in 1759, and again in 1772 after the death of her second husband. She spent the end of her life in Bethlem Hospital[28], dying there in 1792. She was buried at Chelsea Hospital alongside other ex-sailors and soldiers, rightfully deserving her place there.

---

[28] Bethlem Royal Hospital was originally a priory founded in London in 1247. The first record of them receiving patients with mental health issues is 1403, and it eventually began to specialise in treating patients with these ills. It picked up the nickname '*Bedlam*' in the fourteenth century, and this has come to mean '*a state of uproar and confusion*'. The hospital is still open to this day, specialising in neurological issues.

10th March 1777 – Fire and Tar

The Royal Navy relies on ships, and ships rely on thousands of men and hundreds of tons of supplies. Any good strategist knows that if you disrupt the supply chain of an enemy then no matter how expensive – or modern – the hardware it can be rendered useless without having to engage them directly.

In the age of sail, when everything was made from wood, hemp, and canvas, the risk of fire in the dockyards was high; especially if sabotage was involved. So much so that committing arson in one of His Majesty's Dockyards was classed as treason and punishable by death.

On March 10th, 1777, the mizzen mast[29] from *HMS Arethusa* was struck down and erected by the main gates to Portsmouth Dockyard. At over sixty-feet high, this was to become the highest gallows ever used and it was deliberately placed in view of as many people as possible to send a message: treason, specifically arson, would not be tolerated.

Thousands gathered to watch as James Aitken, a twenty-four your old Scottish man, was hung from the top of the mast. A jobbing painter, he had had several brushes with the law already and fled to America in the early 1770's to make his fortune. This didn't work out as he hoped, and in 1775 the American Revolutionary War[30] broke out, with those pesky Yanks wanting independence from Britain[31].

Aitken found himself back in England and devised a plan that, in his eyes, would make him a hero in America, bringing him riches and rewards. If he could set fire to the Royal Navy's dockyards it would hamper their ability to conduct operations off the coasts of North America, including the movement of troops. He could expect to be well-rewarded if he succeeded in his aims.

He created a device consisting of an enclosed candle sitting on a perforated tin containing turpentine and tar, giving him a time-delayed ignition source. By placing the device amongst the highly flammable hemp ropes, the turpentine and tar mixture would act as an accelerant to quickly establish an unquenchable fire.

---

[29] The mizzenmast on a ship is the one nearest the stern, the mainmast is central, and the foremast is the one nearest the bow.

[30] 1775 to 1783, when George III *'lost the American colonies.'*

[31] The *Kingdom of Great Britain* was formed in 1707, with the *United Kingdom of Great Britain and Ireland* formed in 1801.

On the night of the 6th of December 1776, Aitken set his device up in a rope storage room in the ropery in Portsmouth dockyard[32] and returned to his lodgings. He had planned to set fire to the guesthouse to create a diversion, but his landlady caught him with the fuses and he fled. Returning to the dockyard, he lit his device, as well as a secondary fire, and fled Portsmouth.

As he left, he could see the flames rising from the ropery, destroying the building completely in the early hours of the 7th of December. Aitken made his way to Plymouth, aiming to burn down their ropery, but the Royal Navy had stepped up security at all the dockyards after the fire in Portsmouth. When the fire was investigated, his ignition device was found, and his landlady handed in the incriminating items he had left behind in his lodgings.

John the Painter

A reward was put up for the man now identified as 'Jack the Painter'[33], which rose to £2,000[34], but he remained one step ahead. He made his way to Bristol, where he managed to set a fire on one of the ships in the harbour and in several warehouses. The fires did not catch and, aware that arson was involved, the citizens formed up to patrol the streets.

With a price on his head, and knowing the outcome if he was caught, Aitken decided to head for Paris – committing one more robbery in Odiham, Hampshire, to

---

[32] Portsmouth dockyard has had several roperies over the years. A wooden one burnt down in 1760 and was rebuilt only to burn down again in 1770. This time they rebuilt it in brick, and it was over a thousand feet long – the roperies in the dockyards were some of the largest brick-built buildings in Europe at the time.

[33] Over the years he had used a variety of aliases, including Jack the Painter, John the Painter, and James Hill.

[34] In today's terms, that is around £250,000. Twenty years later, a Lieutenant in the Royal Navy onboard a first-rate could expect to earn around £8 per month. Note that common sailors did not get a wage increase at all between 1658 and 1797! It took the mutinies at the Nore (in the Thames Estuary) and Spithead for them to get a pay rise.

raise the money he needed for the ticket. The local jailer saw him acting suspiciously and, realising he matched the description of the wanted miscreant, took him into custody. Amongst Aitken's possessions was a French passport[35] and turpentine, but that was not enough to condemn him. Whilst in custody, a painter named John Baldwin visited him regularly, gaining his trust, and Aitken told him of all the crimes he had committed. Unfortunately for Aitken, Baldwin was an informant and relayed this information to the officials, allowing a court to convict Aitken of treason.

Aitken was taken back to Portsmouth and on March 10th, 1777, was hung from the newly erected mast. His body was then taken down, covered in pitch to preserve it, and placed in a gibbet hung from Fort Blockhouse (*below*), at the entrance to Portsmouth Harbour, where it remained for all to see for many years.[36]

"Above the entrance to the Harbor of this town there stands upon the Gibbet a most piteous set of remains, being the last mortal pieces of a most heinous Criminal, lately caught in these parts..." Lars D.H. Hedbor, The Break

---

[35] Passports were originally '*safe-conduct*' documents, usually issued by royalty - Henry V was granting them in 1414. There is a document known as a passport, signed by Charles I and dated 1641, still in existence. There are similar French ones dating to the reign of Louis XIV in 1667. The word passport is believed to derive from the French '*passeporte*', a pass through the *porte*, or gate, of a city.

[36] Legend has it that his head was eventually removed and placed into the wall of a nearby building in Gosport, though this is just a tale.

29th August 1782 – George Goes Down

The maintenance of wooden ships is an ongoing, and oft-times tricky task. There is an old Royal Navy saying, *"if it moves salute it, if it doesn't paint it"*, and keeping crews busy and the ships in top condition was as much a priority as training on the guns.

Prior to the 1760's, the hulls of ships were not covered with copper plates[37], leaving them vulnerable to the attacks of barnacles, gribble worms, and *Teredo Navalis* (*below*), the naval shipworm. These creatures bore through the external timbers of the ship, weakening them to the point of failure if not countered, and several ships have been lost at sea due to their activities[38].

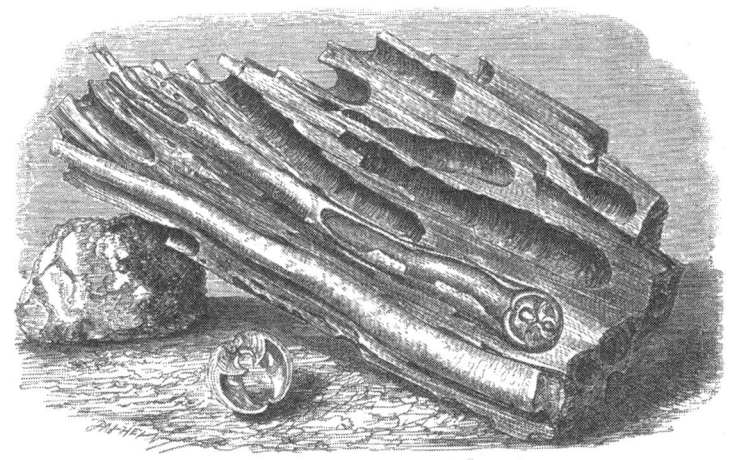

SHIP-WORM.—*Teredo navalis*

To clean and repair the hull requires one of two options. Firstly, you can take the ship into a dry-dock, allowing you full access to the hull in a managed environment, but this is time-consuming and takes the ship completely out of action. The second, and more risky option, is *careening*, where you adjust the centre-of-gravity of the

---

[37] It was 1761 when the Royal Navy started using copper to line the hulls of ships to help protect them, though it did not become standard practice overnight. Take *HMS Victory*, which was constructed by 1765 – she did not get her bottom coppered until 1780. It is also where the expression '*copper-bottomed*' comes from, meaning something safe or protected.

[38] They do not just attack ships. At the start of the 1730's the wooden pilings that protected the earthen Dutch dykes from sea erosion were found to be riddled with seaworms, threatening a major disaster. If the breakers failed then the dykes were in danger of being washed away, which would flood large areas of the Netherlands. New dykes were designed and implemented over the next ten years to replace the wooden pilings with stone slopes.

ship to one side, so the opposite side rises high out of the water, allowing the sailors to work on the undersides of the ship. When you have finished on one side, you move the ballast to the opposite side and repeat the process. This is also used when having to make repairs to areas below the waterline and is known as a 'Parliament heel'.

Moving the centre-of-gravity includes moving the shot, the stores, and even the guns, and it must be a carefully managed operation to ensure the ship doesn't tilt too far, which would dip the gunports below the waterline allowing the sea to flood in (think the *Mary Rose*).

On the 29th August, 1782, *HMS Royal George (below)* was anchored at Spithead, the safe anchorage point in the Solent half-way between Portsmouth and the Isle of Wight. She was thirty-six years old at this point and had been thoroughly exposed to the rigors of the sea, as well as the toll from the three major actions she had fought in.

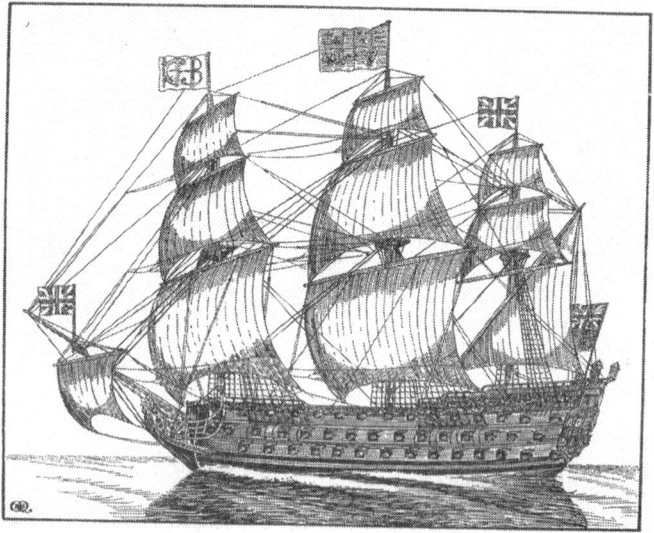

She was slightly smaller than the current *HMS Victory*, which was floated out[39] nine years after the *George* in 1765, but was still classed as a first-rate[40] carrying

---

[39] '*Floating out*' is when a ship is built in a dry dock and the dry dock is flooded, allowing the newly constructed ship to float out, rather than being built and launched into the water from a slipway.

[40] In 1677, the Royal Navy fixed the way they named their classes of ships. This system had several modifications over the years but by the Napoleonic Wars a first-rate had 100+ guns, a second-rate 80 to 98 guns, a third-rate 64 to 80 guns, and a fourth-rate 50 to 60 guns. Anything

100 guns. Onboard were over 1,200 souls – not just sailors and marines, but also families and *"ladies from the Point"*[41]. When ships anchored at Spithead, small boats known as bumboats[42] would take relatives, traders, fresh goods, and the prostitutes, out to them, collecting them before the ships set sail.

That was why, on the morning of the 29th, the *George* found herself with three or four-hundred more onboard than she would when sailing. She was preparing to join a fleet led by Admiral Richard Howe to get an aid column through to Gibraltar when the carpenter reported that a water-pipe a few feet below the waterline on the starboard side needed repairing.

Bringing seawater into the ship was very important, not for drinking but for cleaning, firefighting, and keeping the guns cool[43]. If you get a chance to visit *HMS Victory* you will see the elm-tree pumps still in place, which provided seawater to each of the gun decks. The *Royal George* was equipped slightly differently, with valves in the hull connected to a cistern in the ship. Once the cistern was filled, the seawater could then be pumped up to the gun decks as required. With the chance of battle ahead, this intake would be needed so the decision was made to heel the ship to larboard[44].

To achieve this, the guns on the larboard side were run-out – so that the barrels were protruding through the gunports – and the guns on the starboard side were hauled-in to the centreline. Other items were moved from starboard to larboard, creating the list the ship needed to expose the starboard side of the hull below the waterline. This is something that had previously been done on the ship without incident, though at the time the hull was in better condition, and she was not carrying anywhere near as many supplies (and people).

Unfortunately, the ship wasn't heeled over far enough, and more weight was moved to larboard. Normal operations continued whilst the ship was being heeled; some of the crew were having their breakfast, stores were being loaded, and the families and traders onboard carried on as they were.

---

smaller were classified as fifth-rate (32 to 44 guns) and sixth-rate (20 to 24 guns) frigates, sloops-of-war (16 to 18 guns), brigs and cutters (4 to 14 guns).

[41] Portsmouth Point, which went by the nickname 'Spice Island' for the wide variety of exotic (and mundane) things that could be sourced there, was well known to the sailors.

[42] Bumboats were small boats used to ferry goods and people between the shore and a ship. These were generally rowed, and some had single masts.

[43] Sailors were generally given beer to drink, as it would stay fresher for far longer than water would in a barrel.

[44] *Larboard* is the old term for *port*. Though '*port*' was being used, it was not until 1844 that the Royal Navy ordered it to be used as standard.

After a third movement of weight inside, water started to come in through the larboard gunports, rapidly increasing the tilt. It is important to note at this point that three key warrant officers – the master, the bosun, and the gunner – were not onboard at this time, still being ashore in Portsmouth. As men who knew the ship intimately, you would have expected them to correct the amount of heel before it was too late.

The carpenter, Thomas Williams, raised the alarm but corrective action was sluggish and eventually too late. There was a victualling barge alongside larboard, which delayed the sinking of the ship as it leant on it, but the weight of the *George* pressing down on it sunk the barge. The *George* went down as well - taking less than eight minutes to sink.

It is impossible to determine exactly how many lives were lost as there was no record of how many people were visiting the ship at the time, but it is estimated that around nine hundred people died, including Rear-Admiral Richard Kempenfelt. At the court martial afterwards[45], the blame was put on the age of the ship rather than human error, though some say it was a whitewash to help preserve people's careers.

Because the ship sunk in a heavily used area, efforts were made to recover the guns and then to destroy the wreck to stop other ships from snagging on it. In 1782, Charles Spalding and his divers retrieved 30 of the 100 guns, and from 1834 the brothers Charles and John Deane recovered another 28 guns. Diving on the wreck was achieved using their own invention, a helmet into which air was pumped through tubes via a pump on a ship above. The Deane brothers also investigated a nearby wreck that was causing problems for fishermen at the time, which proved to be the *Mary Rose*, though her location was later lost until 1971.

From 1839 through to 1842, Sir Charles Pasley dived on the wreck to recover as much as possible and to destroy whatever remains posed a danger to shipping. He salvaged a further 30 guns, bringing the total raised to 88 of the 100 onboard.

The loss of the *Royal George* had a profound effect on Portsmouth, with so many locals having been onboard when she foundered. There is a memorial garden on Ryde seafront on the Isle of Wight as many bodies washed up on the shore there[46].

---

[45] Held in the great cabin of *HMS Warspite*, a 74-gun third-rate that was in Portsmouth Harbour at the time.

[46] As well as at Bembridge on the Isle of Wight, and along the shores of Portsea Island.

24th July 1797 – Cold Steel

Tenerife, off the coast of Morocco, is a favoured holiday destination for many, and was an important place for the Spanish after they captured it in 1496[47]. It was a central point for their trade with the Americas, providing a place for ships to re-supply before heading to Spain with the gold, silver, and other goods they carried. It also provided a safe port for Spanish warships.

The British had long found this to be a pain, and in 1797 plans were drawn-up to take the fort at Santa Cruz, in hope of forcing the governor there to surrender. Any ships sheltering in the port at the time could be captured, relieving the Spanish of any treasures they were carrying, which would greatly help the British war effort. The task was given to a newly promoted Rear-Admiral of the Blue[48], one Horatio Nelson, who was on blockade duty off Cadiz. He was given three third-rate ships of the line – *HMS Theseus*, *HMS Culloden*, and *HMS Zealous*, each carrying 74 guns – with *Theseus* being his flagship for the operation. Also in support were the frigates *HMS Seahorse* (38 guns), *HMS Emerald* (36 guns), and *HMS Terpsichore* (32 guns), and two smaller vessels.

The original plan called for the Royal Navy to land 4,000 troops supplied by the army, but the army refused to back this so Nelson and Admiral John Jervis[49] – the newly appointed Earl St. Vincent – decided that the job could be done with the sailors and marines onboard the ships. The marines at that time were '*His Majesty's Marine Forces*', it would be another five years before they would be called the '*Royal Marines*'.[50]

---

[47] The earliest settlers of Tenerife are believed to be the Berbers in around 200 BCE. It took Spain multiple attempts over 30 years to capture Tenerife, the last of the Canary Islands to fall to them.

[48] From 1558, the Royal Navy had three squadrons - the red, the blue, and the white – with the red also being the Admiral of the Fleet. By 1797, the promotion order was Rear-Admiral of the Blue, Rear-Admiral of the White, Rear-Admiral of the Red, Vice-Admiral of the Blue, Vice-Admiral of the White, Vice-Admiral of the Red, Admiral of the Blue, Admiral of the White, Admiral of the Fleet (still with a red squadron flag). From 1805, after Trafalgar, an Admiral of the Red was added before Admiral of the Fleet.

[49] Jervis is regarded as Nelson's mentor and upset several with his favoritism towards him. Vice-Admiral John Orde raised a complaint against this favoritism, but his disagreement was with Jervis's attitude rather than Nelson being in the spotlight – despite some describing him as Nelson's enemy.

[50] His Majesty's Marine Forces were first formed in 1664 as the '*Honourable Artillery Company the Duke of York and Albany's Maritime Regiment of Foot*'. The French equivalent, the '*Compagnies Ordinaires de la Mer*', were formed in 1622 by Cardinal Richelieu, and the Spanish '*Infantería de Marina*' were formed in 1537, giving them the honour of the oldest

Even without the army, Nelson had a force of around 4,000 men at his command, and on July 15th, 1797, he took his ships from the main fleet off Cadiz and sailed for Tenerife, arriving on July 21st, where he landed around 1,000 troops on a beach near the fort. Things did not go to plan, with the terrain working against the invading force as well as the Spanish artillery, and they were forced to withdraw back to the ships. Another plan was needed.

Believing there would only be around 300 defenders, Nelson decided to launch an assault directly on the town, with the ship's boats landing his forces at the port. The Spanish, including their militia, had closer to 1,700, and were well prepared for the attack having guessed Nelson's next move.

On the evening of the 24th, the boats left the British ships to land the troops but came under heavy fire. Determined not to let this attack fail, Nelson himself accompanied the troops to lead and inspire them. The cutter he was in made it to the beach and the troops at the front began to disembark, with Nelson at the rear waiting for his turn.

His next words were, *"I am shot through the elbow!"* (*right*). A musket ball had penetrated his right arm, just above the elbow, shattering it and severing an artery.

Luckily for Nelson, the man next to him had the presence of mind to make a tourniquet from a neckerchief to stem the flow of blood, undoubtedly saving Nelson's life.

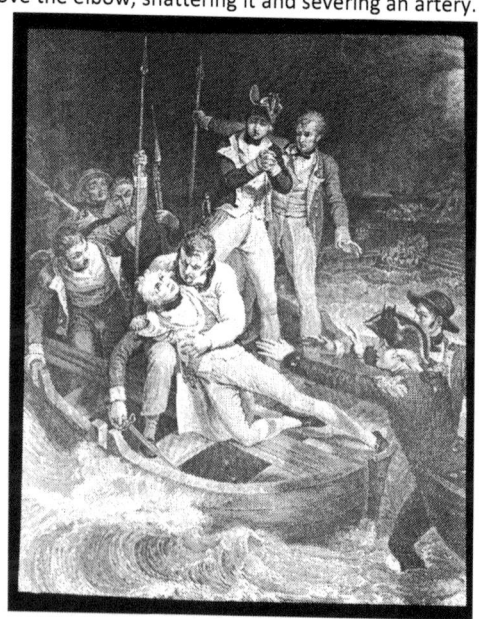

The boat headed to *Seahorse*, but Nelson knew that Captain Thomas Fremantle had his wife onboard at the time[51] and ordered his men to take him to *Theseus* to save the lady from distress.

Onboard *Theseus* it fell to the surgeon, Thomas Eshelby, to do what he could for Nelson.

---

marine corps in the world. The United States Marines Corps were founded in 1775 as the 'Continental Marines'.

[51] See the section on Hannah Snell in 1797 for more information about women on ships at the time.

Even to Nelson it was obvious that there was only one way to proceed, and the surgeon amputated the right arm just above the elbow. There was no pain-relief for the operation, yet the only thing Nelson complained about during the procedure was that the knife cutting his flesh was cold – he actually asked for amputation knives to be placed in warm water in future to save his men the same discomfort[52].

Within an hour Nelson was back at work, concerned for his men still involved in the assault on the town, which by now had reached a stalemate. Captain Thomas Troubridge of *Culloden* and Captain Samuel Hood[53] of *Zealous* were still with the troops in the port and took matters into their own hands.

Hood was sent by Troubridge to see the governor of Santa Cruz, and an agreement was reached that the British would depart – they had threatened to fire the town if the Spanish came at them again – on the promise they would never return. To help discourage any future attacks, the governor let slip into the conversation that there were over 8,000 Spanish troops on the island, five times the actual number.

The British cleared the area, suffering losses of around 250 killed and 120 injured, and never captured a treasure ship in the operation, so it was a failure on all points. Nelson, having lost his dominant hand, had to retrain himself to use his left hand to write with, and there are many examples of his writing before and after the amputation.

Three British Admirals have been defeated at Santa Cruz de Tenerife, and the badge for the town has three lion heads on it (*right*). One for Admiral Robert Blake in 1657, one for Admiral John Jennings in 1706, and one for Nelson.

And the man with the neckerchief who stemmed the flow of Nelson's blood? It was Josiah Nisbet, his stepson from his marriage to Fanny Nisbet[54].

---

[52] Nelson would nickname his stump '*his fin*'.

[53] After whom the famous *HMS Hood* would be named nearly 120 years later.

[54] Nelson had married Fanny (Frances) Woolward in Nevis in 1787, though they never had any children. Her first husband, Josiah Nisbet, died in 1781. Their only child, named Josiah, was born in 1780.

19th October 1798 – The Impregnable Fails

You've spent weeks escorting a group of lumbering merchantmen from Lisbon to the English Channel, crossing the angry Bay of Biscay in October. Upon reaching the Isle of Wight, the merchantmen run ahead to Portsmouth to unload their precious cargoes, but your crew have been somewhat slovenly, and your ship is lagging. A quick look to stern and you see a storm front bearing down – it seems the weather gods are angry. Now you are faced with a decision; do you anchor and ride the storm out or, in your eagerness to get home, try and outrun it to reach the safety of port?

On the 19th of October 1798, that was the question for the crew of *HMS Impregnable*, a 98-gun second-rate that had been launched twelve years earlier. Captain Jonathan Falknor trusted his ship's master[55], Michael Jenkins, who believed they could outrun the storm and reach the safety of Portsmouth. However, this was ill-judged and the ship came too close to the Chichester Shoals, off Dunnose on the Isle of Wight.

The storm pushed the ship onto the shoals, forcing the crew to cut away the masts to lighten the ship and lessen the risk of her turning over. As the night progressed, the incessant pounding on the ship pushed her further and further onto the shoals, and she travelled some two miles across them, severely damaging the hull in the process.

Luckily, all the crew were rescued, but the ship was too far onto the mud flats and too damaged to be saved. Eleven days later, onboard *HMS Gladiator*, a court-martial was held, trying the captain, his officers, and the master. The captain and his officers were honourably acquitted, with all the blame being placed onto Michael Jenkins. He was dismissed from the Royal Navy, but the Navy still had a problem – they were a large warship short for the protection of the Channel, and the French Revolutionary Wars (1792 to 1802) were ongoing.

It would take at least three years to build a replacement, and the navy needed something sooner, so they looked around their harbours to see what ships could be pressed back into service. Once a warship had finished its useful fighting life,

---

[55] The ship's master was a warrant officer responsible for the navigation of the ship, the maintenance of the sails and rigging, and ensuring the ship was correctly ballasted and '*on an even keel*'.

they were often used as receiving ships[56], hospital ships, prison hulks, and storage hulks, floating in the various ports around the country such as Chatham, Devonport, and Portsmouth.

On the River Medway, near Chatham, they found an old first-rate that for the last two years had been used as a hospital ship. It had been earmarked to be converted into a prison hulk, but that had been delayed as once that action was taken the ship could never be refitted as a fighting ship again (or only at an astronomical cost). The surveyors went aboard this ship and estimated it would take six months to refit and get her ready for service. In 1800 she went into dry dock for the refit to begin.

As they stripped away old and rotten timbers, they quickly realised the ship would need far more work than anticipated, and it took three years rather than the envisaged six months. It also cost more than it had to build the ship originally in 1765!

At the end of the refit, the Royal Navy now had a 104-gun first-rate ready for the fight, but the tactical situation had changed. Rather than becoming part of the Channel fleet she was sent to join the Mediterranean Fleet, where the Vice-Admiral there took her as his flagship. For two years the ship proved her worth, and on October 21st, 1805, she took part in the Battle of Trafalgar.

If the master of *HMS Impregnable* had anchored before the storm, then that hospital ship would no doubt have become a prison hulk, and then ultimately broken up. Had that been the case, then Vice-Admiral Horatio Nelson would not have been on *HMS Victory* at Trafalgar, for that was the ship that had been saved (*right*).

---

[56] Receiving ships were introduced to temporarily house sailors before they were assigned to the ship they would serve in. Here, they could be checked for signs of disease or infection, issued new clothes, and the ships also served as floating infirmaries.

3rd February 1804 – An Extreme Row

In 1829, the very first boat race was held between Oxford and Cambridge Colleges along the River Thames, with a challenging distance of just over 4 miles. However that is nothing to what Lieutenant Robert Carthew Reynolds and his men achieved twenty-five years earlier in 1804.

At the time, the French held Martinique and they had sent the recently built *Le Curieux* to Fort-de-France[57] to finish her fitting out. When ready she could then threaten British interests in the West Indies. This caused some alarm to Commodore Samuel Hood (who we met briefly at Tenerife in 1797 when he was only a Captain), who had been tasked with patrolling the area and keeping the French at bay, but Fort-de-France had strong fortifications protecting the harbour so there was no way the British could do anything about the ship whilst it was in port.

Le Curieux, of 16 guns, was anchored under the protection of Fort Saint Louis[58] in a seemingly safe anchorage. In a port held by the Royal Navy, there would always be at least one boat patrolling the harbour at night, regardless of how close the enemy were, but the British officers discovered the French had no such patrols, meaning it might be possible to sneak a raiding party in under the cover of darkness. The problem was if Hood and his ship, *HMS Centaur*, came too near, she would be easily spotted and the alarm raised in the defending fort.

Now, sailors and Royal Marines are a hardy breed and months – if not years – at sea with everything done by hand instils a toughness, but the task Commander Hood set them was of another level. He would anchor the *Centaur* out of sight of Fort Royal, then send four boats with sixty sailors and twelve marines to cut the ship out; board it, overpower the crew, cut the mooring cables[59], and sail it away.

The men were led by Lieutenant Carthew Reynolds, and the distance the seventy-two men rowed was twenty miles just to get to *Le Curieux*! As they approached the stern of the ship at around 1 a.m., they headed for a rope-ladder dangling there –

---

[57] Also known as Fort Royal.

[58] Which the British knew as Fort Edward.

[59] Rope is made from three strands of hemp fibres twisted together, shroud-laid rope is made from five strands, hawsers from nine strands and cable from twelve strands. Cables were used for anchors, being the strongest, and shroud-laid rope for the stays that support the masts. An anchor cable would be 100 fathoms (or 600 feet) long, and on the largest ships would have a diameter of 24 inches.

which would enable them to board the ship much more easily - then they were spotted.

A couple of the guns at the stern of the ship[60] were already loaded with grapeshot, and these were fired at the approaching boats, but the Royal Marines used their muskets to take pot shots at the defenders, keeping them from reloading. The boats came alongside *Le Curieux*, and the sailors and marines boarded, cutting away the anti-boarding netting as they went.

In short shrift, the French on the deck were overpowered, and once you have control of the top deck it is a lot easier to keep the men on the lower decks subdued using half-pikes and bayonets. The French surrendered, and despite incoming fire from the defending forts, the British cut the mooring cables and sailed the ship out, joining the *Centaur* offshore.

Only nine of the seventy-two British were injured, though Lieutenant Reynolds was amongst them and succumbed to his wounds seven months later. The French suffered ten killed and thirty injured, and in an act of kindness – and possibly to rub salt into the wounds[61] – *Le Curieux* was sailed back into Fort-de-France under a flag of truce, where the French wounded and prisoners were released.

HMS Curieux taking the privateer Dame Ernouf, 1805

The newly renamed *HMS Curieux* would serve the Royal Navy in the West Indies until September 22nd, 1809, when she hit submerged rocks. All her crew were rescued and her stores were removed, then the ship was fired to prevent her from being taken back by the French.

---

[60] Guns fired from the stern are called stern chasers.

[61] *'Rubbing salt into the wounds'* comes from when sailors would be given a small pot of salt after receiving a lashing from the cat-o-nine-tails. To help the open wounds heal the sailors would rub this salt into their damaged flesh.

3rd June 1805 – A Stone Frigate Falls

Just off the coast of Martinique, in the West Indies, juts a large basalt outcropping, topping out at just under 575 feet high. It is pretty unremarkable, but its location just two miles offshore makes it an ideal place for keeping a watch on shipping (*below*), and if you put some guns on it you can control a large area of sea.

THE BRITISH FLYING SQUADRON PASSING THE DIAMOND ROCK, OFF MARTINIQUE.

The French had claimed Martinique in 1635 – it is still part of their Republic – and was key to the French Navy operating in that area during the age of sail. In 1803, Commodore Samuel Hood (*right, him again*) was given the job of blockading the key ports of Martinique to tie-up French ships operating there to restrict their income from trade.

Whilst in the area, sailors from his ships would visit the outcropping where they collected callaloo, which when boiled was likened to spinach and helped to fend off scurvy. Between actions, Hood and his first lieutenant took it upon themselves to investigate the rock further, and upon reaching the top they realised how good a view it provided.

At the start of 1804, caves that were already present on the island were adapted for accommodation and storage, and areas for guns were prepared. Using lines from the ships to the rock, the crews hauled two 18lb guns, three 24 lb guns[62], and one 24lb carronade[63] onto the island, where they were set-up in the emplacements. Once complete, Hood named the rock the sloop-of-war *HMS Diamond*, and it was manned by one-hundred-and-twenty sailors and Royal Marines.

So now he had far-reaching eyes, and enemy ship movements could be signalled to his ships from the rock. It was a permanent irritation to the French having a Royal Navy base of operations so close to their ports – and even if Hood sailed his ships away, he still maintained a threat with the guns on the island.

The Royal Navy held the rock for the next seventeen months, harassing ships and generally being a pain in the butt. Several half-hearted attempts were made by the French to recapture it, but all failed, leaving the British sitting pretty. Meanwhile in Europe, the rock had caught the attention of one man: Napoleon Bonaparte. At the time he was creating his grand plan to eliminate or distract the British fleets so he could enact a crossing of the English Channel to invade England. The plan was complex and involved a combined Franco-Spanish fleet sailing from Toulon, picking up various ships on

their way to the West Indies and in the process drawing the British fleets away from the Mediterranean, the North Atlantic, and the English Channel. To invade

---

[62] A 24lb gun and carriage would weigh around two-and-a-half tons.

[63] Carronades were short-barrelled guns for use at close range. Because of the short-barrel they sacrificed range but weighed as much as two-thirds less than a standard gun of the equivalent shot weight. They were manufactured so that the shot diameter was a very close fit to the barrel, giving the shot more force on impact. They also had a sliding carriage to absorb the recoil, meaning the gun did not need to be re-aligned between shots and they could be manned with fewer crew. The first ones were created by the Carron Company in Falkirk, Scotland, hence the name.

England, primarily from Boulogne, Napoleon needed at least three days with no interference from the Royal Navy and he hoped a major action in the West Indies would provide a distraction.

On March 20th, 1805, Admiral Villeneuve[64] (*previous page*) set sail with eleven warships from Toulon, heading for the West Indies. In the process, he had managed to give Vice-Admiral Nelson the slip, giving himself a head start. The complexity of Napoleon's plan and the vagaries of the weather meant that Villeneuve failed to meet up with all the ships he was expecting[65], but he arrived at Martinique on May 14th and joined up with five Spanish ships under the command of Frederico Gravina.

From the 16th of May, the Combined Fleet blockaded the rock and bombarded it, stopping supplies from coming in or out. The attackers managed to sink five small gunboats, and on the 31st of May French troops set foot on the rock. With their freshwater cistern damaged and no supplies left, the defenders had no choice but to surrender – which they did on the 3rd of June – and the French obliterated all traces of the emplacements.

Villeneuve set sail from Martinque, though the plan to join up with other ships went awry and by October of that year he found himself and his fleet holed up in Cadiz. They left Cadiz on October 20th, and on October 21st – after a chase of seven months – Vice-Admiral Nelson finally caught up with them. The battle that ensued was the Battle of Trafalgar.

There is a poem by Henry H. Breen, published in 1849, about Diamond Rock which you can find at the end of this book in Appendix A.

---

[64] Pierre-Charles-Jean-Baptiste-Silvestre de Villeneuve was born in 1763 to an aristocratic family. During the French Revolution (1789 – 1799) he sympathised with the revolutionaries and dropped the '*de*' from his name (the '*de*' translates to '*of*' and is an indicator - but not a guarantee - of an aristocratic background). This allowed him to escape the guillotine, which so many of his fellow naval officers met with as they were also of aristocratic families. Unfortunately, after the defeat of the Combined Fleet at Trafalgar in 1805, fate caught up with him in Rennes in 1806. The official verdict was suicide, but with seven stab wounds to the chest - that seems a little excessive. Many (including myself) believe that Napoleon ordered his execution in a "*who will rid me of this troublesome admiral*" moment, furious after the loss of the fleet. There is no written evidence to back this up, but Napoleon tended to do away with those who displeased him.

[65] Napoleon was superb at planning troop movements on land, including the supply lines required and calculating times it would take to cross different terrain. Movements at sea however frustrated him as the same journey could take two days or a week, depending on the wind direction.

21st October 1805 – Confiding in Your Expectations

On the morning of the 21st ^{of} October, 1805, twenty-seven British warships approached thirty-three French and Spanish ships just south of Cadiz[66]. The first shots were fired at noon, and by tea-time, the battle was over. To complicate matters, a large storm was developing which would smash through the battered ships indiscriminately.

The event would become known as the Battle of Trafalgar, named after the headland[67] near where it took place, and is Britain's best known naval victory. Leading the British fleet was Vice-Admiral Lord Nelson[68], who was killed during the action, but before the fighting began, he wanted to send a message to inspire his men.

The message, of course, was *'England Expects Every Man Will Do His Duty'* and was sent using signal flags. At the time, there were two dictionaries allowing words, phrases, and commands to be issued using a numeric code. Each ship was also assigned a flag, and complex instructions could be given telling ships which position to sail in, who to attack, and so forth.

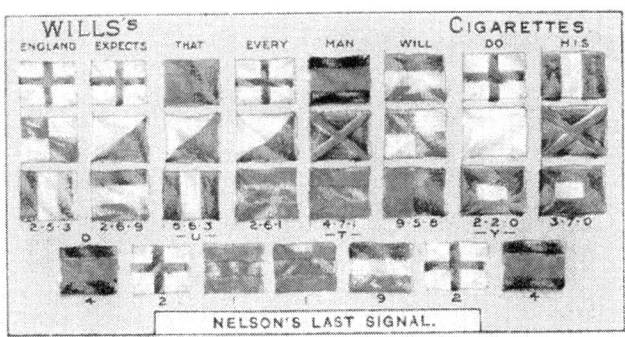

---

[66] The British also had six support ships of 36 guns or less, and the Combined Fleet had seven support ships of 40 guns or less. These were mainly used for passing orders, transferring sailors and marines, and trying to tow dis-masted ships out of the way of the fighting.

[67] Cabo Trafalgar in Spanish, and it should be pronounced more like Traff-al-guh.

[68] Nelson was Vice-Admiral of the White by Trafalgar, and you may start to wonder now about butterflies, in particular the Red Admiral and the White Admiral. As the butterflies have a swathe of their named colour on their wings, it has been suggested that they look like the signal flags an Admiral would fly onboard his flagship, hence the name for the butterflies. There are also references, at around the same time in the late 1600's and early 1700's, of them being called Red/White Admirables rather than Admirals, so I don't think we'll ever have the definitive origin unless some more lepidopterology source material is found.

As you can see above, code 253 equals *ENGLAND* and code 261 equals *EVERY*, whereas *DUTY* had to be spelt out using seven flags as it was not in *Popham's Telegraphic Dictionary*[69].

Though now famous, this was not the original signal Nelson intended – he wanted to send *'England confides every man will do his duty'*, but John Pasco, his signals officer, would have had to spell out confides as well as duty, increasing the number of flags required, so he suggested swapping *confides* for *expects*, which was in the dictionary.

'Confides' meant entrusts, but is rarely used in that form nowadays, whereas *'expects'* still has the same meaning, so it was a good choice by Pasco. The signal is flown every year from *HMS Victory* on the anniversary of the Battle of Trafalgar, the only ship from that battle to still survive.

In 1949, there was another intact ship from Trafalgar, *HMS Implacable* (*below*). She was a French ship, originally launched as the *Duguay-Trouin* in 1800, but was captured on the 3rd of November 1805, after escaping during the action at Trafalgar. She was pressed into service with the Royal Navy and renamed *Implacable*, serving in the Baltic, the Bay of Biscay, and the Mediterranean.

---

[69] Admiral Home Popham first published his signals dictionary in 1799, and it was revised three times through to 1816. It contains hundreds of common words and instructions, for example *biscuit* was coded with the numeric *flags* 1113, *broadside* 1130, *chase* 153, *journal* 142, *persuade* 615, *raft* 1689, *remain* 716, *ravine* 1750, *surgeon* 842, and *useless* 1924, allowing complex phrases to be sent.

After some years in ordinary[70], she was turned into a training ship based off Plymouth, and in 1912 was a training ship off Falmouth for cadets. By 1949 she was in a poor state of repair and no longer needed. The Admiralty, already having *HMS Victory*, decided they did not want to spend any money to repair and maintain her and offered her to the French as a museum ship. The French, still trying to rebuild their shattered country after World War II did not have the funds either, and there were questions as to whether the ship could even make the voyage across the channel.

The decision was made to scuttle her and she was towed out of Portsmouth harbour, passing her old adversary *HMS Victory*, and then scuttled in the English Channel. Her final moments were filmed by British Pathé and you can find the footage on YouTube if you search for *HMS Implacable*.

16th May 1811 – A Presidential Affair

On the 18th of June 1812, the United States declared war on the United Kingdom and her allies. Tensions between the two had been rising for many years, with two key issues relating to the sea. Firstly, the British restricted American trade with Europe, both to boost their own Empire aspirations and to ensure their enemies in the war in Europe (the French Revolution which was quickly followed by the Napoleonic Wars) did not benefit from the traded goods.

The second reason was impressment. The Royal Navy needed huge amounts of sailors to keep their fleets manned and impressment, with the use of the *'press gang'*, allowed them to seize men. The common portrayal of gangs of Royal Marines roaming the likes of Portsmouth and Plymouth and just seizing people from the pubs is somewhat over-hyped – the most common source of crews was taking them from non-navy ships as the Royal Navy wanted men with sailing experience, not just anyone.

There were two types of press, and the standard one had various restrictions[71] which meant they could not take men from merchant ships that were leaving port. They could however take sailors from merchant ships as they returned to port, so

---

[70] *'In ordinary'* is when the ship is effectively mothballed, having guns, sails, yards, and masts removed. A skeleton crew is kept onboard for basic maintenance. The ship can then be repaired or scrapped in the future as required (or re-used as a hospital ship, prison hulk, etc.).

[71] Only those aged between 18 and 55 could be seized, officers and foreigners were exempt. Also, anyone who owed more than £20 could not be seized.

just as a man might be seeing his home in the distance for the first time in months, the Royal Navy might pull your ship over and impress you. You could then be away for years – if you survived the fighting, accidents, and disease.

From 1795 the Quota System was introduced, where every county had to provide a certain number of men. The counties often offered a bonus to men who signed up this way in an attempt to supply the required numbers, but they also used convicts to make-up any shortfall.

When the Royal Navy were really short of manpower, the 'hot press' was used and the restrictions (which were often ignored) went completely out of the window. Nobody would be safe from the press gangs then, even those with a Certificate of Protection.

The Americans introduced their own Certificate of Protection, which said the bearer was an American citizen and therefore exempt from any form of impressment, but the British belief was that your place of birth over-ruled citizenship, so if you were born under the rule of George III you should be beholden to the King.

The estimates of the number of American sailors impressed between 1793 and 1812 varies considerably, but it is somewhere in the region of nine to fifteen thousand! Naturally the Americans were getting rather upset by this, and with the restrictions of trade on their rapidly growing country.

In early 1811 there were several incidents that raised tensions further, and one of those involved USS President[72]. Fifteen days earlier, on the 1st of May, the frigate HMS Guerriere had forced the much smaller USS Spitfire to heave to, after which they impressed one of the crew. Not wanting to lose any more of their own sailors to the Royal Navy, the Americans ordered its own frigates, including President, to patrol the coasts.

USS President was sailing towards New York when she sighted a ship in the distance. Thinking it was HMS Guerriere, she set off after it and what followed next was a series of misidentifications and miscommunications. Commodore John Rodgers[73] of the President believed he was chasing down Guerriere, which was

---

[72] USS President was launched in 1800 and weighed just over 1,500 tons. She was armed with thirty-two 24lb guns, twenty-two 42lb carronades, and one 18lb gun. She was classed as a 'heavy frigate'.

[73] Rodgers would help with the liberation of Washington in 1814 after British forces burnt key buildings – including the U.S. Capitol building and the White House. His son became an Admiral, and his grandson also served in the navy; both were called John Rodgers and there have been six ships named after them in the U.S. Navy.

carrying the recently impressed man from *USS Spitfire*, but in reality, he was chasing *HMS Little Belt*, a much smaller sloop-of-war which carried 20 guns, rather than the 38 carried by *Guerriere*[74].

The captain of *Little Belt*, Arthur Bingham, believed the larger American ship was manoeuvring to attack, so kept trying to tack away. After a chase of around ten hours, the two ships were in hailing range of each other, but the surviving accounts of what happened next contradict each other. The American account says they hailed the British ship first, and the British account say they hailed the American ship first. Then a shot was fired, and again the accounts differ, saying the other side fired first, but this triggered a fierce battle between the two.

The British sloop was a third the size of the American frigate, so it was not an even contest. After fifteen minutes of fighting *Little Belt* was badly damaged and could barely return fire. Captain Rogers ordered a ceasefire, then enquired of the British if they had struck their colours (surrendered). Bingham's response was no, but now the mistaken identity was realised and, rather than re-engage, *President* withdrew, allowing *Little Belt* to make her way back to Halifax for repairs.

The arguments between the two sides continued for months, with the British asking for – but not receiving – reparations for the damage caused by *President*. This left both sides grumbling about the affair, and when war broke out the following year, there was one final reference to it.

On the 19th of August 1812, two months into the war, *USS Constitution*[75] spied a ship in the distance and started to close on her. They quickly identified her as a British frigate and prepared for action. As they drew nearer, painted onto her foretopsail were the words '*Not the Little Belt*'. It was in fact *HMS Guerriere*, and she wanted everyone to know who she was.

Unfortunately for her, she was outgunned by *Constitution*, which was a heavy-frigate, and *Guerriere* was forced to surrender. Too damaged to take as a prize, the Americans fired the ship.

---

[74] *HMS Little Belt* was originally a Danish warship, *Lillebælt*, seized by the British in 1807 after the Battle of Copenhagen (not the one Nelson was involved in). She was renamed '*Little Belt*' and was eventually broken up in 1819.

[75] The *USS Constitution* is the oldest commissioned ship in the world still afloat, docked in Charleston, Massachusetts. *HMS Victory* is the oldest commissioned ship in the world still existing. She was commissioned 11 years prior to *Constitution* in 1778, though her construction was finished 13 years earlier in 1765.

1812 Who needs Ikea?

On the 10th of September, 1813, during the War of 1812 (which in reality lasted for nearly three years[76]) the Battle of Lake Erie took place. The Great Lakes were important for both sides as they were ideal for transporting troops and supplies quickly around Canada and the northern American states, and when war broke out both sides had warships on the lakes in their respective territories.

These ships were nothing like the behemoths that fought at Trafalgar, these were mainly schooners and brigs, with the largest carrying no more than twenty guns and weighing less than five-hundred tons. Britain had bases at York and Kingston on Lake Ontario, and Amherstburg for Lake Erie, whilst the Americans had Sackett's Harbour for Lake Ontario and one on Lake Erie. When war was declared on the 18th of June 1812, both sides quickly began building new vessels as the Lakes were inaccessible from the sea.

The Battle of Lake Erie saw six British ships take on nine American ships, and it was a complete victory for the Americans, capturing all the British ships and losing none of their own. Their commander was Master Commandant Oliver Perry, who is now one of the United States naval heroes, and he received a Congressional Gold Medal for his actions that day[77]. This left Britain with a problem: although there was plenty of lumber in the area for building new ships, there weren't the facilities like there were back in England.

In December of 1813, the Admiralty found a solution for the problem, and orders were sent to Chatham dockyard in England – they were to build a 38-gun frigate, but in a flatpack form that could then be shipped to North America to be assembled there. They decided this was such a good idea that the following month they increased the order to two frigates of 38-guns and two brigs. The frigates were to be called *HMS Psyche* and *HMS Prompte*, with the brigs named *HMS Goshawk* and *HMS Colibri*.

They were only building the frames of the ships, which would then be transported to be assembled at their destination, leaving the planking, decking, masts and rigging to come from local materials. The frames were shipped to Montreal in

---

[76] The War of 1812 started on the 18th of June 1812, and ended on the 17th of February 1815.

[77] At the time of writing there have been 173 recipients of this medal, which is awarded by Congress rather than the U.S. President. The first was awarded in 1776 to George Washington, whilst the most recent posthumously in 2023 to Emmett Till and Mamie Till-Mobley to *"honor the legacy of Emmett Till and the incredible suffering and equally incredible courage, resilience, and efforts of Mamie Till-Mobley that led to the civil rights movement that began in the 1950s."*

March of 1814, but there were no available transports to take the frames on to Kingston where the ships could be built. The limited dockyard at Kingston also had two ships under construction so had neither the space nor resources to start assembling these new ones.

Eventually the frames for *HMS Psyche* were shipped to Kingston and, once a space was cleared, construction began. The shipwright at Kingston, Thomas Strickland, changed the plans for the ship and used the frames that had arrived as the basis for a larger ship. On the 25th of December, the new *HMS Psyche* was launched, but instead of the proposed 38-guns she carried 54. With the war ending just two months later, the flat-pack ship never saw action and the others were never assembled.

22nd September 1835 – A Ship of Stone

Tucked away in a corner of Portsmouth dockyard, England, is a large rock, quite round and un-remarkable. Then you discover the rock has come from the Labrador coast and you realise there is something more to it.

HMS Pique (*right*) was a fifth-rate frigate launched at Chatham on the 21st of July 1834. Powered by sail[78], she was a new design of ship to be used for testing the latest developments in naval warfare, and the following year she found herself under the command of Captain Henry John Rous in the Strait of Belle Isle,

Player's Cigarettes

H.M. Frigate "Pique"

which lies between Newfoundland and Labrador, Canada.

---

[78] Although steam was starting to be used on smaller Royal Navy ships, it would be another three years before their first steam frigate, *HMS Gorgon*, was launched.

On the evening of September 22nd, 1835, she was in the Straits with a freshening wind, so the studding sails[79] were ordered to be taken in. At 10.30 p.m., breakers were sighted ahead of the ship and, though they tried to turn, it was too late - the ship wedged herself onto uncharted rocks and could not be freed.

Overnight, the crew lightened her load, throwing overboard 20 of her guns (very expensive), most of her shot, and around 100 tons of fresh water for the sailors was pumped out. The following morning, as the ship lifted with the changing tide, the men used the capstans to haul on anchors they had put down, pulling the ship free from the rocks.

They limped into the nearby Ance Au Loup cove, where they effected temporary repairs, before setting back out to sea. Once more the wind picked up, and the battered ship had her rudder torn off by the rough seas. Two temporary rudders were tried, but both failed and the ship now found herself facing a crossing of some 1,400 miles across the North Atlantic with no rudder, and a hull that was taking in three feet of water an hour. Surely the ship, and her crew, were doomed?

On the morning of the 12th of October, 20 days after she had hit the rocks, *Pique* limped into St. Helen's Roads, an anchorage off the Isle of Wight. She was taken into drydock in Portsmouth and the shipwrights could not believe the damage they saw once the water was pumped out - crowds of people came to see the miracle ship. Her false keel had been ripped off entirely[80], and her forefoot, which connects the stem and the keel at the front of the ship, lost. An average of eight inches of the actual keel had been torn off along the length of it, and just behind her foremast on the port side was a hole thirteen feet across. On the same side, towards the centre of the ship was another hole, though not quite so large and deep, and towards the rear of the ship was a third hole, this one around sixteen feet in diameter and penetrating the ship.

---

[79] Studding sails, also known as stun'sls, are extra sails that are attached to booms extending from the yards. They are only used in light winds as they place a lot of extra pressure on the masts and rigging.

[80] A sacrificial layer of wood over the keel to protect the structural integrity of the ship should she run aground.

A court martial was held for the officers involved, but they were exonerated, as they should have been. To cross the Atlantic using only sails to steer, having to pump the ship out continuously for three weeks[81] and having barely any keel left was a masterful example of seamanship and determination, both from the officers and the crew. HMS Pique was repaired and put back into service, and it was not until 1910 that the tough little ship was finally broken up for scrap.

One side note for HMS Pique – in 1840 she was involved in the bombardment of Acre (known as Akko, now in north-east Israel) during the Egyptian-Ottoman War. It is estimated some 48,000 rounds were fired from British ships into Acre and the fortifications protecting it, and in 2012 three round-shot were extracted from the walls of the El-Shazliya Mosque. These shot were analysed, both in composition and their location in the wall, and it is believed these three shot were fired from HMS Pique and had been stuck in the wall for over 170 years!

And the rock that you can see in Portsmouth dockyard (previous page)? This rock was found to be plugging one of the holes in the hull of HMS Pique, and it had somehow stayed embedded in the ship as it made its way back across the Atlantic. If it had fallen out at any stage, unplugging the hole, then surely the ship would have foundered.

3rd April 1845 – A Naval Tug of War

By the turn of the 19th Century, a change was creeping into the Royal Navy. With steam engines being used to power sawmills in the dockyards, and then the small tugs in the harbours, it was inevitable they would make their way onto the larger warships.

HMS Comet was launched in 1822. She was one-hundred-and-fifteen feet long and powered by a twin-cylinder steam engine producing around 80 horsepower. She had paddle wheels, which are not the most efficient means of propelling a ship through water – especially in rough weather when a paddle wheel on the port-side of a ship may be cutting through the water but the one on the starboard-side may have been lifted clear as the ship rolls.

---

[81] Working the chain pumps was considered by sailors to be the worst job on a ship. It involves constantly turning a crank handle, with between eight and ten men to a bar and up to eight bars depending on the size of the pumps. Four hours of constantly bending as you worked the handles is not good for the back!

Between 1830 and 1836, four inventors all proposed using a propellor rather than paddle wheels, which caught the eye of the Royal Navy. If you could equip a ship with a propellor, then not only should it increase the efficiency of the engine it also made the machinery less vulnerable, with paddle wheels taking up large, exposed areas on each side of the ship. In 1839, the steam-ship *SS Archimedes*[82] was launched, proving the viability of a screw in use at sea, but the Admiralty still needed to be convinced.

In 1845, a test was devised to see which was more efficient, paddlewheels or a propellor, and they tasked two similar sloops for the test. *HMS Alecto* had paddlewheels and *HMS Rattler* was fitted with a propellor. They tied the two ships together at the stern and held a tug-of-war (*above*).

It was no contest. The propellor-driven *Ratler* pulled the *Alecto* backwards at a rate of 2.8 knots (just over three miles an hour) – a decisive win for the propellor. From then on, ships were built using propellors. In 1906, *HMS Dreadnought* was launched, the first of her kind, and her four propellors each had a diameter of eight feet and ten inches![83]

WILLS'S CIGARETTES.

---

[82] She was not a warship, but the Admiralty tasked her with several speed and efficiency trials. She was also loaned out to the Great Western Steamship Company where Isambard Kingdom Brunel tested her with different propeller designs, leading to propellers being used on the *SS Great Britain.*

[83] The propellors on the *Queen Elizabeth* class aircraft carriers have a diameter of 22 feet and weigh in at 33 tonnes each.

8th June 1897 – False Information

Information is key to the military, and how that information is interpreted and acted upon is equally important. By 1890, the 'Great Game'[84] had been underway for sixty years, where Britain and Russia were at loggerheads over expansionism. Britain feared that Russian expansion would not stop with Central Asia which in turn would threaten their interests in India, whereas the Russians were aggrieved by British influence in the area. There were various conflicts by proxy over the years in the areas of Afghanistan and Persia, but the Crimean War of 1853 to 1856 saw the two come head-to-head with the British supporting the Ottoman empire against Russia.

In 1890, Britain learnt of Russia's plans to build two new cruisers, the *Rurik* and the *Rossiya*. This new class of ship caused consternation in the Admiralty, and to the British public, as they were long-range commerce raiders which could threaten British trade-routes. The Admiralty needed an answer to this potential threat, and the proposed ships would have to be larger than any existing to carry the amount of coal[85] needed to chase down and fight the new threat, if the need arose.

The design they settled on was the *Powerful* class[86], and two were built between 1894 and 1898, HMS Powerful (*next page*) and HMS Terrible. The largest warships in the world at the time, they came in at thirty percent larger than the new Russian cruisers with a displacement of 14,200 tons.

The ships were manned by a crew of 894, and the forty-eight boilers that provided the steam to their two triple-expansion steam engines gave them a top speed of twenty-two knots, four knots faster than the ships they were built to counter. They were twice the size of the previous cruiser class for the Royal Navy, the *Edgar* class, which meant they also cost twice as much. Under a standard load-out they had a range of seven thousand nautical miles, but this could be increased to twelve thousand if all the void spaces were loaded with extra coal.

---

[84] Known by the Russians as the '*Tournament of Shadows*'.

[85] Smaller British warships, such as the destroyers, started being built to use oil rather than coal from 1904. It was not until late 1911 that they started ordering the battleships to be powered by oil. Oil gives ships a better range and faster speeds, but there were also supply problems within the British Empire at the time that made the Navy reluctant to move away from coal, which was readily available.

[86] The first ship in a new class of ships is (nearly) always named after the class, so *HMS Powerful* and *Powerful* class, *HMS Queen Elizabeth* is a *Queen Elizabeth* class aircraft carrier, etc.

The feared conflict with the Russians never materialised and the Navy found itself with two very large and very expensive ships on their hands. Not only had they been costly to build, but they were also expensive to crew and maintain, and the Admiralty was taking the view that having more ships of a smaller size was preferable to fewer large ones.

The two ships eventually found a use to land troops to aid Mafeking during the Second Boer War (1899 – 1902), and some of *Terrible's* guns were used in the Relief of Ladysmith (*see 1899*). Both ships had refits between 1902 and 1904, but were then placed into reserve, their running costs proving just too high. *Powerful* was scrapped in 1929, and *Terrible* was used as a troop-transport during World War I before being scrapped in 1932. They were generally regarded as white elephants; at the time of their launch no other nation could afford – or wanted – to build and run ships of a similar size, and they never encountered the threat they were built for. From the intelligence they received, the Admiralty had over-estimated the capabilities of the Russian cruisers and their over-engineering of the *Powerful* class proved to be an expensive folly.

1899 – Lord Nelson at the Siege of Mafeking

In 1899, Colonel Robert Baden-Powell turned up in Mafeking, South Africa[87], with the aim of raising troops and supplies to defend the borders with the Boer states of the Orange Free State and the Transvaal. Although Mafeking was connected to the railway, it was still relatively isolated, so when the Second Boer War started on the 11th of October that year, Mafeking found itself under siege just two days later.

Improvements to the defences of the town had been undertaken, with gun emplacements, walls, and trenches built in advance of the siege, but the two-thousand men inside were not prepared for the length of time they were entrapped. They held off the besieging forces for 217 days, when a relief column led by Colonel Bryan Mahon fought their way into Mafeking on the 17th of May, 1900[88].

Baden-Powell employed every tactic he knew to protect the town, with everything possible being pressed into service in one role or another, including building a gun out of old steel tubes. As they were scavenging, they came across a partially buried old British 10lb naval gun[89], which was being used as a gatepost.

Originally cast by Bailey and Pegg in 1770, it had been presented to the local Barolong tribe, before falling out of use. The besieged forces excavated it, cleaned it up and pressed it into service. Despite its age and previous usage, it performed admirably, so much so it was given the nickname *Lord Nelson*. Hence Nelson – and a Royal Navy gun – were at the Siege of Mafeking ninety-five years after his death.

Baden-Powell joined the army in 1876, and in 1899 finished his book *"Aids to Scouting"*. It is important to note that scouting here is used in the military term, i.e., spying on your enemy, mapping the land, observation, and critical reporting. In 1907, he held a camp for boys on Brownsea Island, Dorset, and in 1908 published *"Scouting for Boys"*. It was this that led to the formation of the Scouts and the Girl Scouts, who became the Girl Guides in 1910.

---

[87] Now called Mafikeng.

[88] Subsequent analysis of the actions at Mafeking strongly indicate that Baden-Powell had sufficient forces (with their more modern weapons) to break the siege himself.

[89] 10lb is the weight of the shot the gun fired.

30th October 1899 – Guns on the Run

The *Grand Military Tournament and Assault-at-Arms* was a five-day event first held in 1880 in Islington, London, involving only representatives from the Army. It featured feats of strength and speed, and, over time, it was expanded to include the Royal Navy, and the Royal Air Force, and the military bands. The initial feats included the tug-of-war and lemon slicing[90].

The first field gun competition appeared in the event in 1907 in commemoration of the events at the Battle of Ladysmith in 1899. Whilst the Siege of Mafeking was underway (*previous entry*), some 380 miles to the south-east another siege was about to begin.

British forces had concentrated at Ladysmith[91], and with Boer armies beginning to encircle the town, Lieutenant General Sir George White decided to act. On the 30th of October 1899, he sent his army brigades out to capture the nearby Pepworth Hill in the aim of preventing Boer artillery from entrenching there. The day did not go well for the army, and they were forced to retreat across the open area between Ladysmith and Pepworth Hill. The Boer artillery caused horrendous casualties on the retreating soldiers, turning it into a rout.

It was at this point the Royal Navy intervened. Six days prior, White had telegraphed Simonstown asking for naval guns to be sent to provide support, and Captain Percy Scott, of *HMS Terrible* (*next page*), had been working on the task of how to remove and adapt naval guns for use on land, especially for moving them across rough terrain. They took two 4.7" guns and four 12lb guns[92] from *HMS Terrible* and *HMS Powerful*, created carriages for them, then shipped them by train to Ladysmith.

Luckily the railway line remained undamaged, and the Royal Navy arrived at Ladysmith as the army were attacking Pepworth Hill. The guns were unloaded and hauled into position, which was done just in time to provide supporting fire for the British troops as they retreated, though the British suffered over 1,200 killed, injured, or captured by the end of the day.

---

[90] This is a little more difficult than it may sound – a lemon is placed on a pole and as you ride past it you must slice it in half with your sword.

[91] Ladysmith is around 140 miles inland, so not somewhere you would expect to find the Royal Navy.

[92] At this point in time, the Royal Navy were mounting guns identified by the diameter of the shell they fired (4.7" in this case) or the weight of the shot they fired (12lb in this case).

Over the next few days Ladysmith was surrounded and the railway cut, but the newly arrived naval guns had a greater range than the Boer artillery so the Naval Brigade of 283 men that accompanied them spent two days manhandling the guns to better vantage points. This was done using oxen and brute force, but once the guns were in position they could keep the enemy guns subdued. A watchtower was built in signalling range of the naval guns, and whenever a Boer artillery position revealed itself by firing, the British guns were guided where to return fire.

Whilst Ladysmith was besieged, General Sir Redvers Buller arrived in Cape Town. His original plan was to take Bloemfontein, and then Pretoria, but with Ladysmith and Kimberley besieged he was forced to change his plan. He split his forces into three[93], taking the main body of troops and fighting his way to Ladysmith. His advance was costly – the British Army was unused to what we would now describe as Guerrilla warfare, where small, highly mobile units made the best use of the terrain, rarely engaging the British head-on. Buller's force was complemented by naval guns from *HMS Forte* under the command of Captain Edward Pitcairn Jones, and it took three attempts to fight their way through. This included having to cross

---

[93] Accompanying one of the forces, as a war correspondent, was Winston Churchill, just 25 at the time. The armoured train he was on was attacked, and Churchill captured. Four weeks later, he escaped from the prison camp in Pretoria he was being held in and made his way some 300 miles via foot and then train to safety. In 1911 Churchill was appointed First Lord of the Admiralty, though he was blamed for the disaster of the Gallipoli Campaign in 1915 and was forced to resign the position. When World War II started, he was re-appointed to the position on the 3rd of September 1939, and he held this until May 1940, when Neville Chamberlain was forced to resign as Prime Minister and Churchill took on the role. Churchill's enjoyment of alcohol is well known – champagne with every lunch, even during World War II – and it is said he took eighteen bottles of whisky with him to Cape Town.

the Tugela River (*below*) as the nearby bridge had been primed by the Boers with explosive charges.

TAKING THE 47 NAVAL GUN ACROSS THE TUGELA.
Drawing by J. Finnemore.

Finally, after holding out for 118 days, Buller's cavalry rode into Ladysmith to relieve the defenders. The defenders had lost 170 men through fighting, and nearly 400 soldiers and civilians through disease – it is estimated Buller suffered close to 5,000 casualties in his attempt to relive Mafeking! When the sailors eventually returned home, they exhibited their guns at the London tournament, which became the Royal Tournament in 1907.

This then developed into the field gun competition, where teams of sailors from different bases and ships competed to disassemble a gun and its support carriage, move the pieces across a series of obstacles (mimicking the terrain they had encountered in South Africa), then re-assemble it and fire a shot, with the first to fire declared the winner.

The Royal Tournament ended in 1999, but *HMS Collingwood*[94] in Fareham still run a yearly gun-run event, with the *Royal Naval Air Station Culdrose*[95] winning it in 2022.

---

[94] *HMS Collingwood* is a shore base which opened in 1940 and is now the largest naval training set-up in Europe. It is the head of the Maritime Warfare School which incorporates the Royal Marines School of Music, the Defence Diving School, the Physical Training School, and the school of Hydrography and Meteorology.

26th December 1915 – Heading Inland

As we've already seen in 1812 in the Great Lakes of North America, the Royal Navy doesn't just operate at sea. In 1915, British and Belgian forces (and their local allies) were fighting the German forces for control of Lake Tanganyika, which had the Belgian Congo on the Western side and German East Africa on the Eastern side. The lake is over four-hundred miles long[96], so presents a formidable barrier to moving troops if you control it.[97]

At the start of World War I, German forces had two warships present on the lake, giving them superiority. It allowed the Germans to move forces across the lake unimpeded and attack targets in the Belgian Congo. To aid the Belgians, the British had sent the Belgians two 12lb guns to arm a ship they were hoping to build[98], but with no safe area to build the ship, the guns were employed as shore defences instead.

The two German warships were the *Hedwig von Wissman*, weighing in at 60 tons, and the *Kingani*, weighing in at 45 tons. The former was armed with a 1.9" quick-loading gun and a 1.5" Hotchkiss revolving cannon, the latter was armed with four small quick-firing pom-pom guns.

By early 1915, it became apparent the Germans were assembling a third, larger ship, *Graf von Götzen*, which would weigh in at around 1,500 tons. She was designed to carry large numbers of troops quickly around the lake, making her an urgent problem for the war effort in the area. The ship had been built in Papenburg, Germany, and then disassembled and shipped to the Lake in around 5,000 crates.

The Royal Navy has never been afraid to use outside consultants where their own expertise and knowledge might be lacking, but on the 21st of April a gentleman turned up at the Admiralty with a plan. He was John R. Lee, who had fought in the Second Boer War but was now a big game hunter. He had seen the German ships on the lakes, and he proposed to the Admiralty that fast motor gunboats be sent to

---

[95] *RNAS Culdrose* is a shore base in Cornwall, England, opened in 1947 and is home to the Fleet Air Arm's Merlin helicopters. Naval Air Squadrons 814, 820, and 824 operate from there, as well as 700X Naval Air Squadron which operates unmanned aerial vehicles (UAV's).

[96] It is the world's longest lake, and the second largest and deepest lake in the world, behind Lake Baikal in Siberia.

[97] It is now bordered by Burundi, Tanzania, Zambia, and the Democratic Republic of Congo.

[98] This should have been the *Baron Dhanis*, which at 1,500 tons would have made her the largest warship on the lake.

Africa, where they could be broken down, transported cross-country, and then reassembled on the Lake before the Germans could act against them.

A plan was drawn up and Lieutenant-Commander Geoffrey Spicer-Simson placed in charge. Spicer-Simpson had been involved in a few scrapes already, including watching his ship, *HMS Niger*[99], being torpedoed whilst he was entertaining guests in a hotel on the seafront at Ramsgate. Some of the other incidents including almost sinking a Royal Navy submarine, grounding his ship, and sinking a small boat by ramming it. This led to one man describing him as *"a man court-martialled for wrecking his own ships, an inveterate liar and a wearer of skirts."*[100]

Despite this, or perhaps the Admiralty just wanted him out of their hair, he was given two motorboats which Spicer-Simson wanted to call '*Cat*' and '*Dog*', which were rejected as suitable names. He did, however, manage to get them called '*Mimi*' and '*Toutou*', which roughly translate from French as... *cat* and *dog*! The two boats were built and tested at the Thorneycroft Yards on the River Thames, before being shipped to Cape Town, South Africa – around 6,000 miles. They were then put aboard a train to Fungurume (another 2,700 miles) where the line ended, but they were still over one-hundred miles short of their destination. The next one-hundred miles took over a month to travel, with the two boats in their cradles being pulled by two steam-tractors (*overleaf*). Every time a gorge or stream was reached, a bridge had to be built to allow the steam-tractors and their tows to cross, and the accompanying men were constantly having to hack the jungle growth to allow passage.

Finally, they reached the next section of railway, which moved them fifteen miles closer, then travelled by river to the next railway line, another two-hundred miles. With varying river levels, the boats had to be hauled through shallow areas and over sandbanks, it wasn't a gentle river cruise! There was one more leg to complete, which luckily for the men was another by rail which gave them a chance to rest. When they arrived at Kalemie on Lake Tanganyika, it took another month to get the boats kitted out and ready for action. On the 22nd of December 1915, *Toutou* was launched – it had taken nearly seven months to get the boats there and ready!

---

[99] *HMS Niger* was an *Alarm*-class torpedo boat, commissioned in 1893, and converted into a minesweeper into 1909. She was sunk on the 11th of November 1914, by *U-12*.
[100] Please remember this was 1914.

Armed Motor-Boats Trek to Lake Tanganyika

An amazing achievement in the East African campaign was the transport of two armed motor-boats, Mimi and Tou Tou, overland from Cape Town to Lake Tanganyika. Axemen cut roads through miles of bush, and seventeen bridges over eighty feet long were built.

On the morning of the 26th, the German ship *Kingani* passed the harbour at Kalemie and *Mimi* and *Toutou* set off in pursuit. With *Kingani* only able to fire forwards, the faster and more agile British boats harried her from the stern. Her resistance lasted only eleven minutes, when a shot killed the *Kingani's* gun crew and she surrendered. She was taken to be repaired, after which she would be re-launched as *HMS Fifi*.

Meanwhile, there was still the *Wissman* to deal with, and it was not until the 9th of February that the chance to engage her arose. This lasted a lot longer, with *Mimi* engaging her first and then *Toutou* arrived on the scene. A shot from *Toutou* knocked the *Wissman's* engine out and she eventually sunk. This engagement had lasted just over three hours.

The *Graf Von Gotzen*, when finished, was not really used, and as the forces against the Germans were increased on the lake – including four floatplanes[101] – the decision was made to scuttle her. In case they returned in force, the engines and key components of the ship were heavily greased so she could be raised and used at a future date. This never happened, though the ship was raised by the Belgians in 1918/1919, but she was sunk by a storm before she could be fully recovered. The British then raised her in 1924 and found that, due to the heavy greasing applied by the Germans, she was still usable.

In 1927 she set sail under her own steam once more, though now christened the *Liemba*, as a passenger and cargo vessel on the Lake. She is still there now (after several refits) and plies her trade on Lake Tanganyika to this day.

There are quite a few other tales to tell from this area - a village on the western side of the lake[102] is where Henry M. Stanley found Dr. Livingstone in 1871 – but there is one that relates directly to the actions just discussed.

In 1935, C.S. Forester[103] wrote a book entitled *'The African Queen'*. The plot of this book involved a British missionary pressing a steamboat into service to attack a large German gunboat on Lake Tanganyika that was stopping British forces from advancing. They arm the ship with torpedoes and attempt an attack on the German boat. I won't reveal any more of the plot, but it was made into a film for which Humphrey Bogart won the 1952 Oscar for Best Actor in a Leading Role for his portrayal as the mechanic of the *African Queen[104]*.

---

[101] Short Type 827 floatplanes, biplanes built by Short Brothers of Belfast, first flew in 1914.

[102] Ujiji, the oldest town in Western Tanzania.

[103] C.S. Forester (1899 to 1966) is perhaps best known for his *'Hornblower'* series, the twelve books about Horatio Hornblower, a fictional officer in the Royal Navy during the Napoleonic Wars.

[104] It also received nominations for Katherine Hepburn (Best Actress), Best Director (John Huston), and Best Screenplay (James Agee/John Huston).

21st May 1915 – Hiding a Submarine

Camouflage is important in the military world, though at sea you are limited as to what you can achieve, and over the years, many tactics have been tried. Some ships disguised themselves as freighters – called Q-ships – to lure submarines to the surface so they could use their hidden guns on them. As submarines carry a limited supply of torpedoes, if they could surface and sink merchant ships with their main gun they can stay out at sea for longer.

In World War I, the 'dazzle' paint scheme was used on ships[105] (*below, HMS M33 in her dazzle scheme at Portsmouth dockyard*). By breaking up the outline of the ship using random geometric shapes, anyone looking at it from a distance should be unable to work out the size, speed, and bearing, making it harder to fire at them accurately.

---

[105] The dazzle scheme was created by Norman Wilkinson, though accreditation to him after the war took some time as the zoologist John Graham Kerr had also proposed a similar system, though his designs were based on more naturally occurring shapes rather than the geometric ones Wilkinson used.

But how do you disguise a submarine? When they are fully submerged, they have the ocean to conceal them, but when surfaced – or they have their periscope up[106] – they are vulnerable. In 1915, an E-Class submarine *HMS E11*, under the command of Lieutenant-Commander Martin Nasmith, found herself ordered into the Dardanelles to support the Allied action there. She entered the Dardanelles on the 19th of May, passing through the allied picket line and then submerging. As she passed through, every time she raised her periscope for navigation checks it left a tell-tale wake, giving the Ottoman forces something to aim for.

She made it through the Straits intact, leaving her free to roam the Sea of Marmara (*below*). Whilst there, and avoiding patrolling warships, she stopped several merchant vessels and inspected their cargoes to ensure they were not shipping war supplies, and it was on the 21st of May that Nasmith had his idea. He lashed one of the small sailing boats they had inspected to the conning tower to allow the submarine to remain at the surface but – hopefully – undetected. This worked, though they did not come across any targets over the next two days and Nasmith eventually made the decision to cut the boat loose.

CONSTANTINOPLE AND THE SEA OF MARMARA

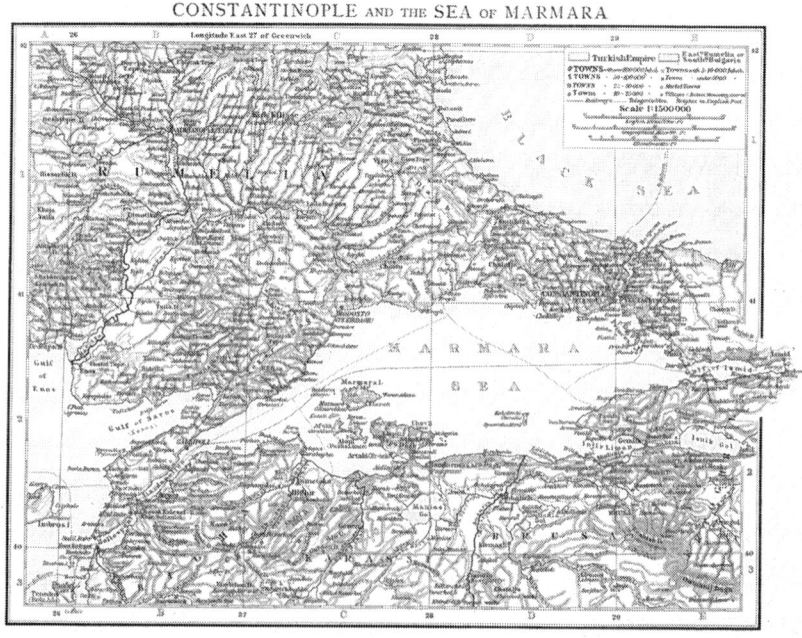

---

[106] Though designs for the snorkel, a tube to the surface that allows it to bring in air for the crew and engines, as well as being an exhaust, along them to stay submerged for longer, was put forward as early as 1916, it was not until World War II that they really began to be used.

On the 23rd of May, *E11* engaged and sank a gunboat, but received damage to her main periscope in the process. The following day, she intercepted a steamer which, though it claimed to be a passenger ship, had a 6″ gun fitted[107]. Once the passengers were escorted off this was sunk by use of demolition charges (rather than wasting a torpedo).

HMS E11 leaving the Dardanelles, cheered on by the crew of HMS Grampus

On the 7th of June, *E11* made her way out of the Dardanelles Strait only to find a mine had become attached to the port hydroplane of the submarine. Fortunately, it did not explode on contact, and by putting the submarine into reverse they managed to free themselves without it detonating. *E11* made two further sorties into the Sea of Marmara, sinking further enemy shipping, and for his actions in the first sortie Nasmith was awarded the Victoria Cross[108], with the following citation:

---

[107] 6″ is the caliber, the diameter, of the bore of the gun barrel, so a 6″ gun fires a shell with a diameter of 6 inches.

[108] The Victoria Cross was first awarded in 1856 for acts of valour committed during the Crimean War (1853 – 1856). The metal for the medals comes from guns captured in previous conflicts (not just the Siege of Sevastopol) and, at the time of writing, 1,358 VC's have been awarded, with three people awarded it twice. Members of the Royal Navy have been awarded 117 VC's. On the 24th of September 1940, Malta was awarded the George Cross, the civilian

"For most conspicuous bravery in command of one of His Majesty's Submarines while operating in the Sea of Marmora. In the face of great danger he succeeded in destroying one large Turkish gunboat, two transports, one ammunition ship and three storeships, in addition to driving one storeship ashore. When he had safely passed the most difficult part of his homeward journey he returned again to torpedo a Turkish transport."

Two officers on *E11* received the Distinguished Service Cross[109], and the ratings were awarded the Distinguished Service Medal[110], with the boat[111] being scrapped in 1921. So, it is possible to camouflage a submarine on the surface, you just need to find yourself a small sailing vessel to do so!

7th June 1917 – Two Become One

Destroyers played an important part for the Royal Navy during World War I, being fast and agile they made excellent platforms for scouting and rapid response. Though only carrying a few guns of relatively small calibre, they also carried torpedo tubes to pack a punch and were the workhorses during the war – the loss of any of them was felt keenly.

From 1905, twelve *Tribal class* destroyers were built, each carrying two 4" guns and two 18" torpedo tubes. They were 255-feet long and powered by oil-heated steam turbines, giving them a top speed of 33 knots[112], and all ended up serving during World War I.

On the night of the 26th of October 1916, one of these destroyers, *HMS Nubian* was involved in a skirmish with German ships in the Dover Straits when she took a torpedo hit towards the front of the ship, badly damaging the bow. After the battle she was taken under tow in an attempt to save the ship, but rough weather caused the tow ropes to break and the ship was driven ashore. She was driven so far onto the shore the navy had to blast a channel through the chalk to re-float her in

---

equivalent of the Victoria Cross, for their heroism in holding out against constant attacks from the Rome-Berlin Axis.

[109] The Distinguished Service Cross was originally the Conspicuous Service Cross, first awarded in 1901 and renamed in 1914. The medal was also awarded to the city of Dunkirk in 1919 for the gallantry of its citizens.

[110] The Distinguished Service Medal was awarded between 1914 and 1993.

[111] Submarines are referred to as boats, rather than ships or vessels. The earliest submarines were lowered into the water and crewed from a tender ship, much like ship's boats, so the name stuck.

[112] 38 mph, 61kmh

another attempt to salvage her, but her bow was lost completely. The wreck was towed into Dover, and then taken up to Chatham dockyard.

Just a few weeks later, on the 8th of November 1916, another *Tribal*-class destroyer, *HMS Zulu* (below), was sailing across the English Channel to Dunkirk when she hit a mine, which had been laid by *SM UC-1*[113]. The mine exploded under the engine room, killing three and completely separating the stern of the ship, which sank. The crew managed to seal the still afloat section of the ship and it was towed to Calais by the French destroyer *Capitaine Mehl*, before being taken to Chatham.

This left the Royal Navy with a problem – they had lost two destroyers in a short space of time and had these two useless lumps of metal sitting around. Someone, whether in the dockyard or in the Admiralty, came up with a great idea - take the back of *Nubian* and the front of *Zulu* and stick them together to make a new ship.

As the two ships were of the same class, it should have been relatively simple, but Nubian had been built at Southampton and Zulu at Tyneside and when they measured them one was 3.5" wider than the other! Despite this, the plan to join them went ahead and just six months later, on the 7th of June 1917, the hybrid ship was launched.

---

[113] *SM UC-1* was a German minelaying submarine that was credited with sinking over forty ships with mines. She had a crew of 14 and on July the 24th, 1917, took a direct hit by a 250lb bomb dropped from a flying boat that penetrated the conning tower, sinking her.

The new ship, christened *HMS Zubian* in honour of her two donors, was attached to the 6th flotilla patrolling the Dover Straits and took part in the First Ostend Raid on the 23rd and 24th of April, 1918, when the Royal Navy was tasked with blocking the ports of Zeebrugge and Ostend. A canal led from each of these ports to Bruges itself, and it was a base of operations for the German Navy for submarines, motor torpedo boats, and small surface raiders. As well as heavy shore fortifications, the area in front of these ports is a maze of channels running between shifting sandbanks.

At Ostend, the raiding force started to bombard the port to provide cover for two old cruisers, *HMS Sirius* and *HMS Brilliant* to get into the main channel. The two cruisers had been stripped of anything useful and their holds filled with concrete and old stone so they could be sunk, blocking access in and out of the port (especially for submarines). The German commander, in a brilliant tactical move, had repositioned the main channel marker buoy into the centre of the sandbanks, meaning the British ships headed straight onto the sands where they made easy targets for the German defences. The blockships were scuttled in the channels by the sandbanks, but not in any place where they could affect the access in and out.

At Zeebrugge, things were different, and it has since been referred to as '*The Greatest Raid*', amongst other nicknames. The events already fill many books, but the plan was to land sailors and Royal Marines from *HMS Vindictive* to take out the German gun emplacements on the mole[114] and use two old submarines filled with explosives to destroy the viaduct that connected it to the mainland. Three old ships – *HMS Thetis, Intrepid,* and *Iphigenia* – would then be taken into the main canal and sunk.

The plan relied on smokescreens laid by the destroyers to cover the approach of the *Vindictive* and the blockships, but the wind changed direction, exposing the oncoming attack force. *Vindictive* landed her troops in the wrong place on the mole, forcing them to face heavy defensive fire as they fought their way to the gun emplacements. One of the submarines, *HMS C1*, grounded before reaching her target so was abandoned, and the other, *HMS C3*[115], was manually steered into the

---

[114] The mole was a stone jetty that curved in a protective arc for nearly a mile around the entrance to the harbour. It had multiple gun emplacements embedded onto it as it was the first line of defence for the port. Any German reinforcements had to cross the viaduct that joined the mole to the mainland.

[115] Both submarines were manned by volunteer crews, who had put their names forward before being told what the mission was.

viaduct and detonated in the correct place[116]. The blockships *Intrepid* and *Iphigenia* made it to the channel where they were sunk.

Later analysis of the raid show that passages were cleared through the sunken ships within a few days, and a secondary route was dredged to allow submarines to enter and leave at high tide. 227 British sailors and Royal Marines lost their lives[117], with 356 wounded, whilst the Germans lost 8 killed and 16 wounded. Eight Victoria Crosses and one-hundred-and-forty-three Distinguished Service Medals were awarded for this action, and there were two-hundred-and-eighty-three '*Mentions in Dispatches*' for other individuals. The 4th Royal Marines Battalion, who were landed from *HMS Vindictive*, took horrendous casualties.

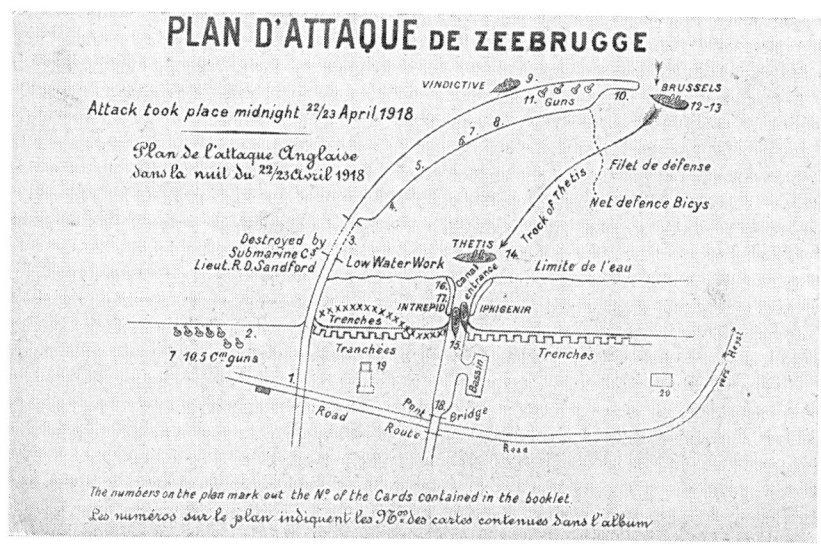

PLAN D'ATTAQUE DE ZEEBRUGGE

I have only skimmed over this action briefly; as mentioned it needs an entire book to try and cover the events of that night and although the outcome was not as effective as hoped, the propaganda that followed for both those at home and the serving troops was invaluable.

A second raid on Ostend was undertaken on the 9th of May, 1918, where *Vindictive (below)* and another ship were sunk as blockade ships. This too was not the complete success the Admiralty needed, but it trapped the larger German ships there for the remaining six months of the war.

---

[116] Once the submarine was in place, the crew used timed fuses to escape before she detonated.

[117] There is still some debate on the number of casualties. Many of the sailors who helped man the ships across the Channel should have boarded boats to take them back to England before the battle, but they hid so they could stay onboard and fight.

One of the most Daring Exploits in Naval History. H.M.S. Vindictive filled with Concrete, Fitted as a Block Ship, and Successfully Sunk across the Entrance of Ostend Harbour, May 10th 1918. To prevent German Submarines from Operating in the Channel.

Our Frankenstein destroyer, *HMS Zubian*, survived the Ostend raid, and the rest of World War I, but was scrapped in December 1919 after the end of hostilities.

31st January 1918 – A Bad Practice

For over a year the German High Seas Fleet had not ventured into the North Sea in any numbers since the Battle of Jutland[118], and the British fleets had started receiving the new *K*-class submarines. Unlike the Germans, the Admiralty wanted submarines to work in conjunction with a fleet, running alongside them at the surface before submerging to engage the enemy once they were spotted.

To this end, Vice-Admiral Richard Beatty organised a large exercise to be conducted by the Grand Fleet on the 1st of February 1918. On the afternoon of the day before, forty ships set sail from Rosyth, on the Firth of Forth, Scotland, heading for Scapa Flow where the exercises were due to take place. The ships included battleships, cruisers, destroyers, and submarines from the 12th and 13th Submarine Flotillas.

---

[118] 31st of May 1916 to the 1st of June 1916.

K-class submarines had numerous issues. They were steam-powered, rather than diesel[119], which meant they had smokestacks and air vents for when they were running on the surface. To dive, the boilers had to be extinguished, the smokestacks lowered into the ship, and the air-vents closed with mechanically operated caps. Any point of failure in these operations meant that the submarine could not dive, and there were often reports of debris floating in the sea sticking in air-vents, meaning they could not be closed. The diesel-powered German submarines could crash-five in around thirty seconds, the British *K*-class took at least five minutes to prepare and then start to dive. As the *K*-class had a very good surface speed – up to 24 knots compared to the German U-boats which made between 14 and 17 knots – the Admiralty believed that if a *K*-class was caught on the surface it could outrun most opponents, rather than dive and hide.

A K-Class submarine, K11, though after the events described here as the bow has been modified with a 'swan-bow' which was added to improve its buoyancy control

As the sun set on the evening on the 31st of January, the British ships sailed out, forming a line nearly fifteen miles long. Radio-silence was enforced, to ensure no German U-boats would detect their presence, and the only lights shown was a single directional blue light at the stern of each ship for the ship behind to follow. At the head of the line was *HMS Courageous*, which was followed by *HMS Ithuriel* and the 13th Submarine Flotilla, consisting of *K11*, *K17*, *K14*, *K12*, and *K22*. Behind them were *HMAS Australia* and three other battlecruisers with their destroyer

---

[119] The Admiralty were still trying to produce diesel engines that would produce sufficient power for submarines at this point and were forced to use steam for the submarines to be able to keep up with the fleet.

escorts, and then came the cruiser *Fearless* and the 12th Submarine Flotilla of *K4*, *K3*, *K6*, and then *K7*. The submarines were running on the surface to ensure they could keep up with the fleet.

They were doing close to twenty knots in the mist, just passing May Island, when *K11* spotted two ships in the distance that were not part of the battle group. *K11* turned to port to avoid them, and she was followed by *K17*. *K14* did not see the ships, and with radio-silence no commands were passed from the leading submarines, so she slowed down rather than follow her sister ships, then she saw the two ships ahead. She turned to port, but the rudder jammed. Forcing her into a continuous port turn. The captain ordered the ship to a stop whilst they tried to free the rudder, and they turned their navigation lights on to indicate to the ships behind that they were dead in the water.

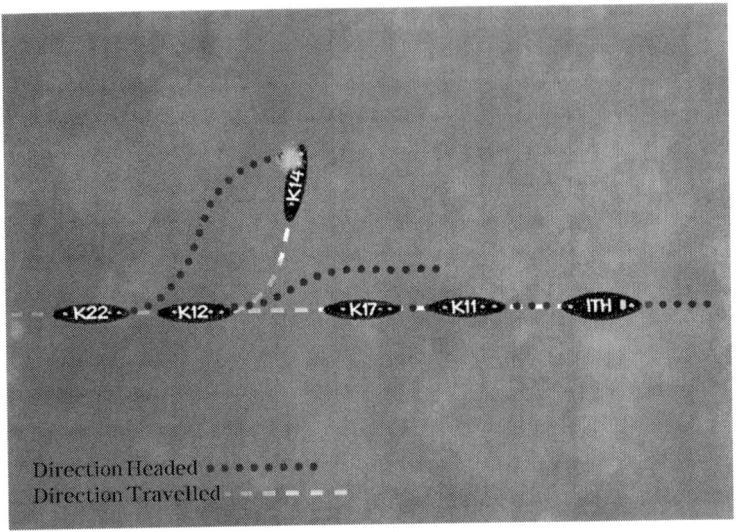

K12 had spotted *K14* and avoided her, but *K22* had lost the tracking light from those ahead and she drifted off course, to port. Unfortunately, this drift took her directly into the path of the beleaguered *K14*. When they spotted *K14* ahead, *K22* tried to avoid her but ended up ramming her, slicing her bow off. Two men on *K14* were killed at this point, and both submarines were taking on water from the impact damage.

You would think that, at this point, it was just an unfortunate error, and though two men had been lost it could have been much worse. Flares were set-off from the stricken boats, and morse-code signals sent using lanterns in the hope that the ships behind would see their distress. *K22* gently reversed out of *K14*, when the giant battlecruisers came up out of the mist. The first three missed, going around the submarines, but *HMS Inflexible* was also out of position and found herself heading towards *K22*. She managed to turn enough to only catch her a glancing blow, but she damaged the ballast tanks and hull along the starboard side.

Another close call, and by now it was becoming clear that there were problems with the submarines in the fleet. Word reached *HMS Ithuriel* nearly half an hour later, and she turned back to assist, ordering a wide turn to starboard so that they would avoid the other ships still coming behind them. The boats all turned at slightly different times, and though they thought they would miss the battlecruisers, they were heading straight for them.

In the mist, *Ithuriel* found herself facing the oncoming HMAS Australia, and turned to starboard so she passed down the side of the much larger ship. *K11* followed *Ithuriel* and missed the *Australia* as well, but *K17* and *K12* did not change course until the very last moment. Remarkably, both managed to avoid an impact, but you now have the *Ithuriel* and the four clumsy submarines with her heading through the battleships, cruisers, and destroyers.

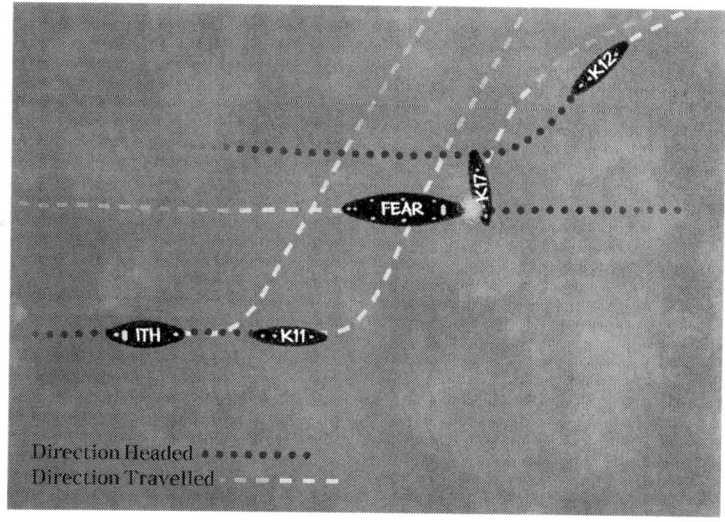

Direction Headed • • • • • • • •
Direction Travelled – – – – – –

And in the middle of them all is the 12th Submarine Flotilla, led by *HMS Fearless*. The general rule of the sea is if a larger vessel is heading towards you, you should be the one to turn to avoid the collision, in theory being the more manoeuvrable vessel. So when *HMS Fearless*, weighing a thousand tons more than the submarines, saw the 13th Flotilla weaving their way through the oncoming ships, she naturally expected them to make action to turn. *K17* didn't, and *Fearless* went through her. A section of bow was torn off from *Fearless*, and she halted to take the men off the doomed *K17*.

K4, behind *Fearless*, stopped safely, and *K3* managed to come to a halt near to Fearless and *K4*. The oncoming *K12* managed to weave through the stopped ships and submarines, before coming round to offer assistance to the crew of *K17*. In a small area, you have the four British submarines and *HMS Fearless*, and there were still two more submarines out there – *K6* and *K7*.

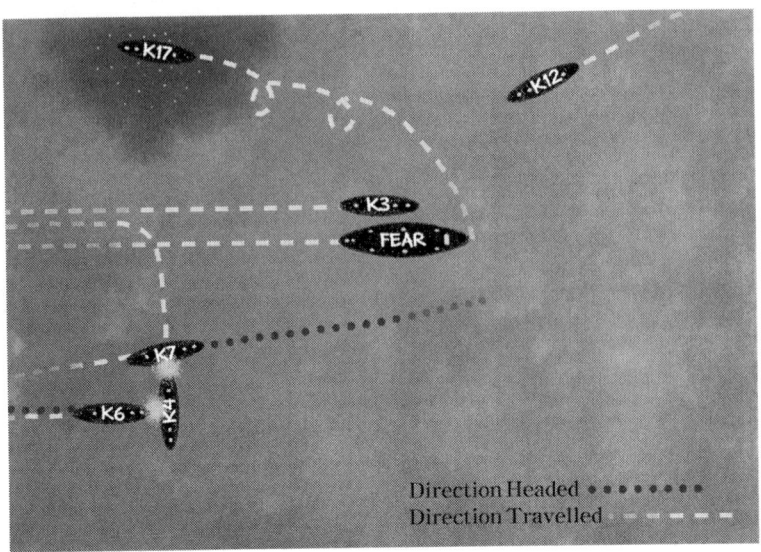

K6 had lost track of the submarine she had been following, when she saw a light in the distance and headed to it at speed to catch up. Unfortunately, it was a light on the stationary *K4* and she hit her amidships. *K4* started to sink from the catastrophic damage, and she was sinking so fast that the approaching *K7* ran over the top of her, only scraping her bottom.

K6 reversed out of the sinking *K4*, saving herself, and set about looking for survivors in the water, but there was one final twist - the remaining battleships and destroyers bearing down on the cluster of crippled and stopped vessels. In the dark and the mist, they remarkably avoided any further collisions, but the wash from the passing ships and their propellors washing over the sailors in the water caused numerous deaths.

In just over an hour, the Royal Navy had lost the submarines *K4* and *K17*, three were damaged (*K6*, *K14*, and *K22*), and *HMS Fearless* would need major work to repair her bow. All fifty-five men aboard *K4* were lost as she sank so rapidly, two died aboard *K14*, and forty-seven died onboard *K17*.

And the two ships that were spotted in the mist at the start of this chaos? They were never identified.

21st June 1919 – Any Old Steel

On the 11th of November 1918, the Armistice was signed[120] and the *'Great War'* was finally over. Four years of conflict had wracked the globe and the victors were now squabbling over the remains of the war machine that Germany and her allies had created. Tanks, guns, and the great fleets were all being eyed, both as war compensation and as a way to quickly re-equip battered forces.

One of the biggest prizes, the German High Seas Fleet, was escorted into the British naval base at Scapa Flow in the Orkney Islands between the 25th and 27th of November. The fleet consisted of seventy-four ships[121] which was made up of eleven battleships, five battlecruisers, eight cruisers, and fifty destroyers, as well as the twenty-thousand men who sailed in them. Interestingly, as the ships were interned rather than captured, the ships were still sovereign property of the German state, so no British (or other nation's) guards could be stationed on them.

Conditions for the German sailors were grim; morale was low, food was rationed, and the postal service that did exist for contact with their homeland was slow and unreliable. It is one thing being on a ship when you have a role to perform, but when you spend months anchored under the watchful eyes of your British captors, it was a trying time for them. There is a critical design difference between German and British ships at this time – British ships had large compartments for their working areas and cabins as they were designed to be able to sail anywhere in the Commonwealth for long periods, whereas German ships were expected to operate relatively close to their homeports, so the internal compartments were smaller, making them cramped for their confined crews.

It is interesting to note that these compartment sizes played a role at the Battle of Jutland in 1916. The battlecruiser *SMS Seydlitz*[122] was hammered during that battle, taking one torpedo hit and twenty-one large-calibre shell hits, yet she still made it back to port. Because of the smaller internal compartments, the flooding was more easily contained, though it still defies belief that she made it back in this state (*below*).

---

[120] The signatories of the Armistice were the Marshal of France, Ferdinand Foch, and the First Sea Lord Admiral Rosslyn Wemyss for the Allies. For Germany, it was signed by Major General Detlof von Winterfeldt of the army and Captain Ernst Vanselow of the navy, and two civilians Count Alfred von Oberndorff and Matthias Erzberger.

[121] The majority of their U-boats had been escorted to Harwich, Essex.

[122] Seiner Majestät Schiff, or *'His Majesty's Ship'*.

Back at Scapa Flow, the sailors were being returned to Germany in batches, so by June of 1919 there were just over four thousand sailors remaining. Meanwhile, at the Paris Peace Conference, the fate of the contested territories and the German fleet were being discussed. All thirty-two Allied countries involved had their own agendas and goals, whether that was the British Empire, Brazil, China, Haiti, Liberia, the United States, and all the others. The Italians and the French both lodged claims for some of the ships to add to their navies, whereas the British wanted them destroyed to remove their threat permanently.

The Germans wanted to go one step further – rather than let any nation benefit by taking the ships, they would scuttle them, denying them to all, and there are communiques from Admiral Hans Hermann Ludwig von Reuter to Germany as early as January of 1919 stating the ships should be scuttled. As the talks in Paris progressed, the German commanders grew increasingly nervous about the fate of the ships, which were still under the watchful eyes of the British naval patrols.

Then, on the 21st of June 1919, the British fleet left Scapa Flow to conduct exercises, the same day that the Treaty of Versailles was originally due to be signed[123]. The German commanders believed that if the treaty was not signed, they would be at war again and, effectively, be sitting ducks as all their ammunition had been removed. They must have been unable to believe their luck when they saw the British forces departing the area that very same morning.

---

[123] The Treaty was finally signed on the 28th of June, but the British had a plan to seize the German ships regardless of the outcome of the treaty on the night of the 23rd of June.

At 10 a.m., once the Royal Navy were clear of the area, Reuter signalled his ships to prepare to scuttle, and at 11.20 a.m. he followed this up with the order to proceed. Across the interned ships, sailors began smashing water pipes, opening the seacocks[124] and portholes.

It takes time for water to enter a ship this way – unlike the large hole a torpedo makes – and it was not until midday that there was a noticeable effect on any of the ships. The first to show was the battleship *Friedrich der Grosse*, which listed to starboard. At around 12.20 p.m., the British officers taking part in the exercise received word that the German ships were sinking and made full steam back to Scapa Flow, but they were too late.

By tea-time, fifteen of the largest ships had sunk, as well as five light cruisers and thirty-two destroyers, two-thirds of the German fleet. For those that had not yet sunk, British ships towed them onto the beaches to stop them from being lost. The German sailors abandoning the ships were picked up but were now treated as prisoners-of-war, though that didn't improve their living conditions as they were interned in camps that were not much better than the ships.

The British were happy that the threat of the ships was gone, as were the Germans knowing the ships would not fall into the hands of those they had fought

---

[124] Seacocks are valves that lead through the hull to the sea, usually used to provide water for firefighting or adding ballast weight.

against, whereas the French were dismayed as they could have used them to instantly rebuild their fleet.

The ships remained sunk for the next four years and then, in 1923, Ernest Cox bought the rights to the destroyers and two of the battlecruisers for a minimal sum and began operations to raise them for salvage. Each destroyer had close to a thousand tons of steel in them, which could be sold on for recycling, and a battlecruiser was twenty-thousand tons or more.

Cox came up with a method of sealing the holes in the ships, then pumping air inside to re-float them; a dangerous and costly job, yet he managed to raise thirty-five ships in total before selling his company and the rights for the remaining ships.

Salvage continued, and by World War II, there were only seven ships left on the bottom, where they remain to this day. Though they are now protected wrecks they still have a value, and not for scrap. They were sunk before the 16th of July, 1945, meaning they were safely underwater when the first nuclear test was carried out in Los Alamos, New Mexico (code name Trinity). The subsequent atom and nuclear bombs that were detonated raised the background radioactivity levels across the globe but had no effect on these sunken ships. This means that any steel salvaged from them does not have these increased levels of radioactivity, no matter how small an increase, making it invaluable for the construction of body-scanners in the health industry, space-based detectors, and Geiger counters.

25th August 1939 – A Naval Nuisance

The Royal Navy has been known to recruit all types of people, especially at times of war when manpower was hard to come by, but in 1939 they took the unusual step of recruiting a dog – a Great Dane in fact.

Benjamin Chaney bought the dog as a pup and took him with him when he went to run the United Services Institute in Simon's Town, South Africa. Sailors coming ashore would feed the dog treats and make a fuss of him, then they started taking him on the train as they went for day trips. When the train guards came round, they would try and hide the dog – not an easy job as on his hind legs he stood over six-and-a-half feet!

The sailors would offer to pay for a ticket for the dog, but the guards did not allow animals on trains and ordered him to be removed at the next stop. *Nuisance*, for this was the name he had earned for himself by this time, would wait for a train heading back and return home.

The train companies became sick of this and petitioned for the dog to be put down unless the sailors stopped him from boarding trains. Naturally this enraged the sailors, and they wrote to the Commander-in-Chief of the Navy demanding action. As Nuisance was held in fond regard by his men, to keep them happy the CiC came up with a plan - by enlisting the dog into the navy he would then, like the sailors, be eligible for free train travel, leaving the train companies unable to do anything.

On the 25th of August 1939, the Great Dane was enlisted: first name *Just*, surname *Nuisance*, trade *Bonecrusher*, religion *Scrounger*, all signed, of course, by a paw print. A seaman was given the daily job of preparing Nuisance for appearances at events, making sure the dog was wearing his specially commissioned hat. He also had his own logbook, with punishments listed. The worst was when he was caught sleeping in a Petty Officer's bed, for which he was denied bones for seven days.

Eventually, a car accident and ill-health caught up with him, and he was euthanised on the 1st of April 1944. He was laid to rest with full military honours, including a bugler playing the *Last Post*, and is buried at Klaver Camp, Simon's Town. In 1985, a statue was erected in Simon's Town to commemorate Nuisance, which can be seen to this day.

16th February 1940 – Pirates in Norway

Say the word *"cutlass"* and pirates spring to mind, but the last definitive use of the cutlass by the Royal Navy was in 1900 during the Boxer Rebellion (1899-1901). The Boxers, so called by the west because the martial arts many practiced were nicknamed 'Chinese boxing', should really be called the Yìhéquán, or the Society of Righteous and Harmonious Fists. Their aim was to remove the foreign influences they saw interfering with, and diminishing, their way of life and their traditions.

The Boxers attacked and destroyed foreign properties, eventually forcing many of the foreigners to take shelter in an area of Peking[125] called the *Legation Quarter*.

---

[125] Now Beijing

Eight nations, including Britain, Russia, the United States, France, and Italy, allied to put down the rebellion and free their besieged citizens, but the Chinese decided to back the Boxers with the Imperial Chinese Army from June 1900.

Control of the mouth of the River Hei and the four forts – called the Taku forts (*below*) – that protected the approaches was critical for the alliance to allow them to land and re-supply troops in the area as they were positioned less than one-hundred miles from the capital. An allied fleet assembled offshore and gave the Chinese forces a deadline to surrender the forts.

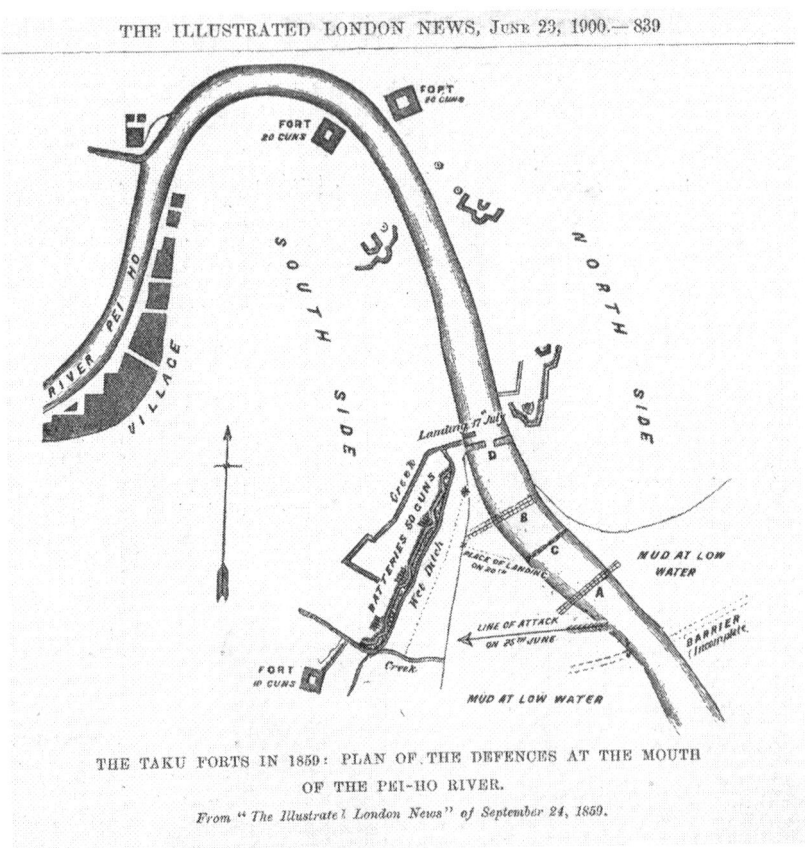

THE ILLUSTRATED LONDON NEWS, June 23, 1900.— 839

THE TAKU FORTS IN 1859: PLAN OF THE DEFENCES AT THE MOUTH
OF THE PEI-HO RIVER.
From "The Illustrated London News" of September 24, 1859.

In the early hours of 17th of June, before the deadline passed, the forts engaged the offshore allied fleet, forcing them to respond. Two British torpedo boat destroyers, *HMS Fame* (*below*) and *HMS Whiting*, approached the docks and were involved in the capture of four Chinese torpedo boat destroyers there. The Chinese destroyers were boarded by Royal Navy crews, and cutlasses were used in this action. The forts were captured shortly afterwards, with the whole action taking less than six hours.

H.M.S. Fame.

But there is a later reference to their use. Though the cutlass was officially withdrawn from issue on the 22nd of October 1936, small ships still carried ten and larger ships carried twenty for ceremonial purposes, so the for the event in question the ship involved would have been carrying them.

In late 1939, the German *Deutschland*-class cruiser[126] *Admiral Graf Spee* was raiding commerce shipping in the Atlantic. Eight Allied groups, including four aircraft carriers, three battleships, and sixteen cruisers, were despatched to find and sink her. She was considered such a threat because of her size and armament – compared to the British heavy cruiser *HMS Exeter*, *Graf Spee* was six-thousand tons heavier, seventy-feet longer, and carried 11" main guns rather than *Exeter's* 8" main guns. A formidable opponent indeed, which is why the Admiralty needed her dealt with.

A cruiser cannot operate for long periods at sea without support, and the Admiralty were sure that one of the ships keeping the *Graf Spee* supplied was the tanker *Altmark*. This ship was indeed fulfilling that role, keeping the cruiser topped up with fuel, food, and ammunition. She was also taking onboard prisoners the

---

[126] There were three ships in this class, the other two being the *Deutschland* and the *Admiral Scheer*. The *Deutschland* was renamed the *Lützow* in 1940 as Adolf Hitler feared the propaganda nightmare that would follow the destruction of a ship named after the homeland. The *Admiral Scheer* was in Kiel harbour in 1945 when it was hit by bombs from an RAF raid, causing her to capsize.

cruiser had captured from the merchant ships. On the 6th of December 1939, 140 prisoners were transferred to the *Altmark*[127], taking the total she carried to 299. Seven days later *Graf Spee* was spotted by *HMS Exeter* and her escorts, leading to battle, and *Altmark* would never meet up with *Graf Spee* again.

The action between the British and German ships became known as the Battle of the River Plate, which resulted in the heavily damaged *Graf Spee* taking shelter in the neutral port of Montevideo, Uruguay, on the 14th of December, 1939. There followed three days of political pressure from both sides on the Uruguayans, who favoured the British side. There was a lot of false information being spread to try and trick the Germans into believing a large force was assembled and waiting for them off the coast, though in reality they were still days away. The Germans also used propaganda claiming mistreatment of prisoners and the bodies of the dead, though these claims have since been proven false.

On the 17th of December the *Admiral Graf Spee* left port, watched by thousands of locals and film-crews. Before it could be engaged or captured by Allied forces, her Captain, Hans Langsdorff[128], had the ship scuttled just outside of the port. All this was filmed, and you can see her leaving port and being scuttled on YouTube: www.youtube.com/watch?v=SWgXQDo-tdQ. This action was the basis for the 1956 film 'The Battle of the River Plate', starring Anthony Quayle and Patrick MacNee.

But what has this to do with the cutlass? *Altmark*, no longer having a ship to supply, began her journey back to Germany. As she was carrying prisoners onboard, the captain opted to go through Norwegian waters, who at this point of the war were neutral. Three times in those waters the Royal Norwegian Navy gave her cursory inspections, but the presence of prisoners was not declared by the Germans (for obvious reasons) and not noticed by the Norwegian inspection parties.

On the 15th of February, 1940, an aircraft on patrol from RAF Thornaby, Yorkshire, spotted the ship and directed *HMS Cossack* to intercept. *Altmark* took refuge in the Jøssingfjord, and initially *Cossack* was prevented by the Norwegian navy from

---

[127] *Graf Spee* had attacked nine commercial ships, including the *SS Clement*, the *SS Newton Beech*, the *SS Ashlea*, the *SS Huntsman*, the *MV Trevanion*, the *African Shell*, the *Doric Star*, the *SS Tairoa*, and the *Streonshalh*. Eight were sunk, whilst the *SS Huntsman* was captured and then scuttled seven days later after her prisoners were transferred to the *Altmark* as there was no space for more prisoners onboard *Graf Spee*.

[128] There is a campaign for Langsdorf to be honoured as rather than lead his crew to certain death if he had taken them out to fight the Allied fleets he scuttled the ship, letting the crew off before she sank. He saved over 1,000 men with this action, but because he refused to continue the fight, defying Hitler's direct orders, no honour or official memorial has been granted. Langsdorf committed suicide three days after the scuttling.

boarding her for inspection. Politics were at play in the background – as they had been at Montevideo – but eventually the captain of *Cossack*, Philip Vian, informed the Norwegians he was going to inspect *Altmark* and they could join him if they liked.

The Norwegians declined, and on the 16th of February, at 10:20 p.m. sailors from the *Cossack* boarded *Altmark*[129]. The Norwegians did not interfere, but the German sailors were desperate to protect their ship and there was a short but fierce struggle. This involved hand-to-hand fighting in which eight Germans were killed and one wounded, whilst the Royal Navy suffered one wounded. Once the ship was under their control, Royal Navy sailors went down to the hold, where they shouted, *"Any Englishmen here?"* When the prisoners responded, the sailors replied, *"Well, the Navy's here!"*

---

[129] Winston Churchill, as First Lord of the Admiralty at the time, personally ordered the Altmark to be boarded.

This became a well-known phrase, becoming the title for a book on the incident and a song, and was used for propaganda purposes. The cutlasses alleged to have been used in the hand-to-hand fighting are believed by some to be the last time the Royal Navy used them in combat and, somewhat appropriately, the Germans erected a sign at the spot where the ship was seized which read, *"Here on 16th February 1940, the Altmark was seized by British Sea Pirates"*. The sign is now on display in the National Museum of the Royal Navy, Portsmouth (*below*).

Members of the *HMS Cossack* Association are not convinced that cutlasses were used during this operation, and the information that they were comes from one sailor who said he saw one being carried aboard the *Altmark* by the boarding party, so we will never know for sure if they were or were not used.

If 1900 is the last date the Royal Navy definitely used them, there is a report from the Royal Australian Navy that on the 11th of September, 1914, at the Battle of Bita Paka, New Britain[130], crews from Australian destroyers used cutlasses in their assault on two German radio positions. It was also at this battle that the Australians suffered their first casualties of World War I.

---

[130] Papa New Guinea

9th December 1942 – One Becomes Two

During World War II, Germany commissioned 568 type VIIC U-boats, their main submarine in the war, and some of their commander's names are still familiar to many. Names such as Otto Kretschmer, who sunk 46 ships, Erich Topp, who sunk 35 ships, and Günther Prien, who sunk 30 ships. Yet many commanders lost their lives, along with their crews, on their first or second sorties and some seventy-five percent of all U-boat commanders died during the war. Across the war, over 28,000 German sailors lost their lives in U-boats, close to seventy percent of those who set to sea.

U-602, commissioned on the 29th of December 1941, was fourteen days into her fourth patrol when she went missing in the Mediterranean sometime after the 19th of April, 1943. Her fate is still unknown, but she is remembered for one of the stranger incidents in World War II.

The previous year, in the Mediterranean, on the 9th of December she sighted and torpedoed *HMS Porcupine*, a Royal Navy *P-Class* destroyer. Seven sailors were killed on *Porcupine*, but remarkably she did not sink despite significant structural damage. The ship was nearly split in two by the force of the explosion and the crew jettisoned as much weight from the ship as possible in a bid to keep her afloat.

This worked, and the ruined ship was towed to Arzew, Algeria[131], where it was clear nothing could be done to save her. Rather than write her off for scrap, the Royal Navy came up with another plan. The ship was separated into two halves at the damaged area and everything useful, including guns were removed. The ends were then sealed, making her watertight, and the two sections towed to Portsmouth, England.

Now you may think there is not a lot you can do with two floating halves of a ship, but the Navy anchored them in Portsmouth Harbour and used them as accommodation blocks. Even though they were not complete, the two sections needed to be named, so with some panache the forward section was christened *HMS Pork*, and the aft section *HMS Pine*. They were eventually scrapped in 1947.

---

[131] The liberation of Algeria had started the month before, on the 8th of November 1942, with '*Operation Torch*'.

2nd September 1942 – Duties for Apes

If you had signed up for the Royal Navy during World War II, there were dozens of different career paths available to you - signal boy, sailmaker (yes, they were still needed then), Ordinary Seaman, wireman, blacksmith, photographer, surgeon, and more.

If you had chosen the medical route were stationed at Gibraltar, you may have found yourself with some unusual patients to look after – Barbary macaques, the famous apes that live on the rock of Gibraltar.

Like the ravens of the Tower of London, there was a belief that if there were no longer apes at Gibraltar it would fall from British possession, having been their territory since it was captured during the War of the Spanish Succession (1701 to 1715) and officially ceded to Great Britain in the Treaty of Utrecht of 1713[132].

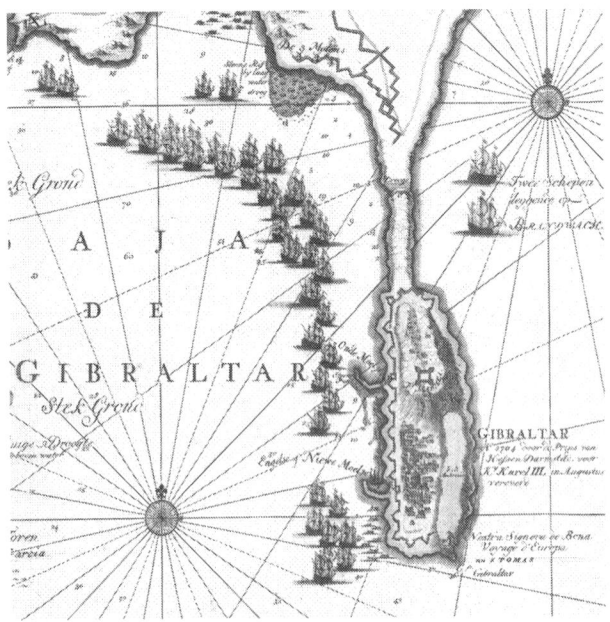

Above, the capture of Gibraltar on the 3rd of August 1704, by Dutch and English ships. Courtesy of the Rijksmuseum (Object RP-P-OB-83.395,15).

---

[132] 13th July 1713, pursuant to Article X of the Treaty of Utrecht, the Spanish Crown ceded to Great Britain *"the town and castle of Gibraltar, together with the port, fortifications, and forts thereunto belonging"*.

Gibraltar is in a position to monitor the flow of traffic through the Straits of Gibraltar, which at its widest is just under nine miles across, so having a base here is strategically important. It has been the subject of many sieges over the years, and despite concerted efforts to drive the British from the rock during World War II, it was never captured or over-run.

In 1913, when the apes on the rock numbered only ten, eight female apes were shipped in from North Africa under the direction of Sir Alexander Godley. He also deemed that the British Army on the island became responsible for the care of them, with an *Officer-in-Charge of the Apes*.

When apes became sick, they were taken to the Royal Naval Hospital, where a junior doctor could end up treating something even hairier than the average able seaman – service in the Royal Navy leads to all sorts of interesting places and situations!

Twice during World War II, extra apes were shipped to the rock to increase the population. In 1942, Churchill himself ordered five females to be added to the troop as the population had fallen to just seven. And, on September 2nd, 1944, he issued an order that the population always be kept at a minimum of twenty-four.

Nowadays, there are around three-hundred apes, and several times small groups have been relocated from Gibraltar to keep their numbers under control. How the apes got there in the first place – as they are of North African origin – has yet to be proved, but the existence of a tunnel from Morocco that goes under the Straits of Gibraltar to the rock has been ruled out, despite the persisting legend of one[133].

---

[133] There are plans for a tunnel to be created between Spain and Morocco that goes under the Straits of Gibraltar, which were first aired in 1979. These plans have recently been raised again, and further studies are being undertaken to see if a tunnel between Tarifa, Spain, and Tangier, Morocco, could be completed.

16th May 1943 – The Navy Inspires a Bounce

The curriculum in education changes frequently, with topics peaking and waning in popularity depending on the thinking of the time. Sometime at the start of the 1900's, a young boy was attending Haberdashers' Aske's Hatcham Boys' Grammar School in New Cross, south-east London, and no doubt was daydreaming out of the window during a history lesson. Something during that lesson must have caught his attention and lodged in his brain, and though he did not know it at the time it would prove to be of importance.

Forty years later, in 1942, the Nazi war machine was in full production, with the Ruhr valley one of the key industrial areas for steel. The power and water for steel production was being controlled by two dams, the Möhne and the Edersee, with additional capacity from the Sorpe dam in the Eder Valley. The War Office needed these dams to be taken out, but conventional bombing would be unable to penetrate the thick concrete constructions. Step forward our schoolboy, now in his fifties and with a career in engineering behind him. He had worked on the *R100* airship, and importantly created the geodetic airframe[134] design which allowed stronger yet lighter airframes in larger aircraft. The most successful plane to use this design was the Vickers Wellington, of which over 11,500 had been produced by the end of World War II.

At the outbreak of war, our engineer started designing new bombs that could penetrate heavily reinforced targets, but unfortunately there were no planes large enough to carry his designs. The largest bomb he proposed was ten tons in weight, and our engineer even designed a plane large enough to carry it. The most lauded bomber of World War II was the Lancaster bomber, which was still two years away from being built at this point. The proposed plane had a wingspan seventy feet longer (172 feet in total), carried six engines not four, and was almost double the weight of the Lancaster – a true behemoth if it had taken to the skies[135]. Without the ten-ton bombs he had dreamt up, or a plane capable of carrying them, our engineer needed another plan.

His alternative plan was to drop a smaller bomb into the water directly behind the dam, where it would sink and act like a mine, detonating underwater. The problem was the lakes contained by the dams all had anti-torpedo netting protecting them

---

[134] Geodetic airframes were made by load-bearing members crossing each other in a spiralling fashion (think of a honeycomb but with four-sides to each cell). The U.S. Navy used a simpler version of this in their heavy frigates, such as the *U.S.S. Constitution*, which can be viewed today if you visit her.

[135] His proposed design was to be called the '*Victory*' bomber.

so torpedoes could not be used, and it would be nigh on impossible to drop a bomb directly down behind the wall – and this is where he remembered his history lesson from all those years ago...

At the Battle of the Nile, back in 1798, the British gunners ricocheted their shot across the surface of the sea at the ships of the French. This could only be done when the sea-state was calm, and when done at close range, it would mean the chance of missing the enemy ship (by going over it) were greatly reduced. To ricochet – or skim – a shot, they would fire the guns on the lowest gun decks at roughly a minus seven-degree angle with a full charge. On impact with the sea, the shot would do exactly as we do now with stones at the beach and bounce along the surface until it hit something or ran out of energy. It also meant that if the shot penetrated, it would be going through the target on the up or on the down angle, meaning it was more likely to cut through multiple decks and do more damage.

NB: Though our engineer was taught it was used at the Battle of the Nile, using ricochet was not new, it had been known – and documented – in 1742 in Benjamin Robins' "New Principle of Gunnery"[136].

Continuing his schoolboy reminiscence, he set to work skimming marbles across a tub of water to develop his idea. In July of 1942, a test mine (though pre-positioned and not dropped from a plane) destroyed the redundant Nant-y-Gro damn in Wales, proving that the idea was sound, if our engineer could get his bomb to work.

Tests of the new bomb took place at Chesil Beach, Dorset, and Reculver, Kent, with most of them failing as they tried to identify the design of the bomb-casing, the height it should be dropped from, and how fast the bomb should be spinning to allow it to bounce correctly. The final test of the bomb, designated 'Upkeep', occurred on the 13th of May, 1943, when a live bomb weighing in at 9,250 pounds[137] was dropped at exactly two-hundred-and-thirty-two miles per hour, from a height of sixty feet, and with a backspin on the bomb of five-hundred revolutions per minute – that is how exact his calculations were! The bomb skipped along the water, covering 720 metres, before sinking and then exploding.

---

[136] There is an earlier publication, '*The Arte of Shooting in Great Ordnance*', from 1587 which mentions ricochet shot to target shore fortifications but using only one bounce so that the shot goes up into the defenders.
[137] 4.625 tons.

Only three days after that final successful test, on the 16th, nineteen Lancaster bombers of 617 Squadron[138], led by Wing Commander Guy Gibson[139], set off from *RAF Scampton*, Lincolnshire, to take out the three dams on '*Operation Chastise*'. Eight aircraft were lost and fifty-three crew were killed, but they succeeded in breaching two of the dams and damaging the third. I'm sure you have realised that our young schoolboy was none other than Barnes Wallis, and the operation is more commonly referred to as the '*Dam Busters*'.

It is important to note that Barnes Wallis[140] was not the only individual who worked on the bouncing bomb and the methods to deliver it, but it was his determination and energy that led to *Operation Chastise* occurring, not to mention the bravery of the crews flying the Lancaster bombers.

How much damage was done to the Nazi war machine is still a matter of contention: the production of steel in the area was severely disrupted for four months, and factories and infrastructure were heavily damaged by the floodwaters. Over sixteen-hundred civilians, many of whom were prisoners-of-war forced to work for the Germans, lost their lives in the flooding. For the British public, it was a major psychological boost, and the effort the Germans put in to repairing the damage meant that the resources were diverted from elsewhere, specifically the defence of France where just thirteen months later D-Day happened.

On the 12th of November 1944, 617 Squadron went after the German battleship *Tirpitz* – sister ship of the *Bismarck* – using Barnes Wallis' '*Tallboy*' bombs. These were closer to his original ten-ton bomb idea, though weighing in at five-tons which could be carried by the Lancaster bomber. *Tirpitz* was holed up in Tromsø Fjord, Norway, and had repelled attacks from X-craft (mini-submersibles) and the air, including a previous attack

---

[138] 617 Squadron was formed on the 21st of March 1943, specifically for this mission. They had only been training together for 56 days when they flew their first operational mission.

[139] Remarkably, Gibson was just 24-years old when picked to lead 617 Squadron. In total, he flew over 170 missions before his death in September the following year. Though he and his crew survived the mission against the dams, none of his crew survived the war. Gibson died in a mission he was flying in a Mosquito, not his familiar Lancaster, which crashed near Steenburgen, Holland.

[140] The 1955 film, '*The Dam Busters*', was not overly kind in their depiction of Barnes Wallis. Although brilliantly acted by Michael Redgrave, he was not quite the bumbling and shabby man as shown – he was just over six-feet tall and was described as having a strong, almost captivating, personality.

using Tallboys that had failed to hit the target[141]. Eighteen Lancaster's from 617 Squadron, thirteen from 9 Squadron, and one from the Royal Australian Air Force to film the results, went after the ship under 'Operation Catechism'. All were stripped down to give them maximum range whilst carrying such a heavy bomb, and after nearly seven hours of flying they found themselves over the target. Two of the massive bombs hit the *Tirpitz*, though one failed to explode, and several exploded in the water near to her, with the shockwaves causing damage to the hull. At 09:52 a.m., the ship capsized, just fourteen minutes after the attack began. There were no losses to the bomber crews, but an estimated twelve hundred lost their life on *Tirpitz*.

It is not the strongest link to the Royal Navy, I admit, but it is an important one and it has been reinforced in the last few years. 617 Squadron[142], the *Dam Busters*[143], were disbanded in 2014, but in 2018 were reformed and now operate out of *RAF Marham*, Norfolk – and are now equipped with the F-35B Lightning II's. These are the new STVOL (Short Take-Off and Vertical Landing) aircraft that operate on the Royal Navy's latest *Queen Elizabeth* class aircraft carriers based out of Portsmouth.

1943 – If It Floats – Use It

Wood is great for building boats and ships, having been used for around ten thousand years. In the mid 1800's, along came iron, then steel, then aluminium alloys, and then fibreglass[144]. Other materials have been experimented with over the years, but perhaps one of the strangest materials is... ice!

In the early years of World War II, there was an area of the Atlantic where Allied air coverage could not protect shipping, called the Mid-Atlantic air gap[145]. It covered approximately six-hundred miles north-to-south and three-hundred miles east-to-west, running pretty much down the middle between North America and

---

[141] She had sustained some damage from these repeated attacks.

[142] 617 Squadron was formed specifically to use the bouncing bombs as they were top secret, and the required training was incredibly demanding. After Operation Chastise, the squadron specialized in precision bombing.

[143] The squadron badge depicts a burst dam, and the motto translates to '*After me, the flood*'. The badge was approved by King George VI in March 1944.

[144] The first warship to use fiberglass for her hull was *HMS Wilton*. Commissioned in 1973, she was a 450-ton minesweeper that was decommissioned in 1994. She is now the headquarters of the Essex Yacht Club at Leigh-on-Sea, Essex.

[145] It was also known as '*the Black Pit*'.

Europe. Allied convoys in this area were extremely vulnerable to U-boat attacks, and the supply lines were critical to the war effort.

With Bomber Command requiring long-range aircraft for their bombing campaigns, such planes were rarely available for Coastal Command to provide air cover for the convoys. Steel was in short supply, ruling out building escort carriers, so another solution was needed.

Ice, either from an iceberg or ice flow, had previously been considered for use as a floating airstrip, with a German scientist experimenting with the idea in 1930. It also popped up in a memorandum at the Admiralty in 1940 but was quickly dismissed. It took Geoffrey Pyke (1894 – 1948) to propose the idea again in 1942, with an 'ice' aircraft carrier nearly two-thousand feet long – huge, coming in at twice the length of the Royal Navy's latest aircraft carrier, HMS Queen Elizabeth[146]. Areas inside would be hollowed out for hangars, storage, accommodation, and all the machinery needed to propel it, steer it, and keep it cold.

In early 1943, a trial model was built in Alberta, Canada, at sixty-feet long, thirty-feet wide, and built around a timber structure. A network of pipes was installed to 'spray' the vessel with cold air, but testing proved that a full-sized version would suffer badly from 'cold flow', where the structure would deform over time. To solve this, it was proposed to cover the hull in insulation and add steel beams for reinforcement – the cost for the proposed carrier was starting to escalate rapidly.

Pyke had come across previous experiments where sawdust was added to water and then frozen, creating a promising material. He worked with Max Ferdinand Perutz, an Austrian scientist who had fled continental Europe to England in 1939, to perfect this material, which was christened Pykrete.

They found that, when frozen, a mixture of 14% sawdust to 86% water was stronger than ice alone and melted far more slowly, giving them a suitable material. The problem now was that changing requirements for the new carrier were coming in thick and fast: it had to have sides 35-feet thick to withstand torpedo hits, the Royal Navy demanded it have a rudder to steer rather than engines on each side, and it would need to have a range of at least 7,000 miles.

---

[146] The Queen Elizabeth class aircraft carriers are the Royal Navy's largest ever warships, coming in at 932 feet long and having a displacement of around 65,000 tons. The largest ship the Royal Navy ever built prior to this was the battleship HMS Vanguard, which had a length of 814 feet and a displacement of 45,200 tons.

By mid-1943, aircraft were being fitted with long-range fuel tanks, extending their patrol range, and baby flat-tops (escort carriers)[147] were being provided by the United States. The Pykrete project was starting to look untenable, and in December 1943 it was finally shelved.

There is one story that Lord Francis Mountbatten took a block of ice and a block of Pykrete into the Quebec Conference of 1943 and fired a shot from a revolver into each. The first one, the ice, shattered, whereas the second shot ricocheted off the Pykrete, almost striking Admiral Ernest King.

1959 – Nuclear London

In 1959 construction started on the Royal Navy's first nuclear-powered submarine[148], *HMS Dreadnought* (S101)[149]. She was to be 265 feet long, carry a crew of one-hundred-and-fifteen, and was armed with six torpedo tubes. Powered by an American-built Westinghouse 78 MWth (Megawatt thermal) S5W reactor[150] which heated water to create steam which drove two steam turbines. She served for nearly twenty years before being decommissioned and is now sitting in a dock at Rosyth, her fate still undecided at the time of writing this[151].

Whilst she was being constructed, the Royal Navy needed to be able to train both their own personnel and civilian engineers on nuclear reactors, so a decision was

---

[147] Before being given to the Royal Navy, one unusual modification had to be made to them – the removal of the ice-cream machines onboard! As the U.S. Navy had been alcohol free ('dry') since July the 1st, 1914, ice-cream had become the replacement treat, and all the U.S. ships carried large supplies of it or the ability to make it themselves. With the Royal Navy still issuing a rum ration (see next section), the ice-cream makers were deemed unnecessary and were removed.

[148] The first nuclear powered submarine was the American *USS Nautilus*, commissioned in 1954.

[149] Oddly enough, the Royal Navy's previous *HMS Dreadnought*, launched in 1915, is the only battleship to have deliberately sunk a submarine. On March the 18th, 1915, *U-29* of the Imperial German Navy was patrolling near the Orkney Islands when it encountered part of the Grand Fleet. They fired a torpedo at *HMS Neptune* (which missed), but this caused the sub to surface. Two British ships, *Dreadnought* and *Temeraire* raced to sink her, with Dreadnought reaching her first. It was no contest, with *Dreadnought* weighing in at around 20,000 tons and *U-29* around 660 tons. *Dreadnought* sliced *U-29* in half, sinking her quickly, and all 35 of the crew perished. In their haste to ram the submarines, both Royal Navy ships had to manoeuvre sharply to avoid colliding with each other.

[150] The second submarine in this class, *HMS Valiant*, was powered by a British-built Rolls-Royce PWR1 nuclear reactor.

[151] There is one plan to take her back to Barrow-in-Furness, Cumbria, where she was built, and open her as a visitor attraction.

taken to build a small 10-kilowatt reactor. Though the unit was only twelve-feet high, it required over three-hundred tons of concrete and steel around it for shielding. As with all things, the reactor was given a name, and this one was called Jason, and if anyone asked about it they were told it was a model, not a real reactor core. The remarkable thing was the nuclear reactor was installed in a building complex designed by Sir Christopher Wren (1632 – 1723) that was completed in 1712 and is now a Grade-1 listed building!

The site? The King William Building at the Old Royal Naval College in Greenwich, just six miles from the centre of London. The reactor went critical (live) in 1962, and the following year Greenwich was declared a nuclear-free zone – the border for the declared zone just happened to run alongside the site, rather than include it.

The reactor operated for over thirty-years until 1996, and the operation to dismantle it and remove the reactor and the 270 tons of radioactive material began. Obviously moving tons of nuclear material, even the low-level waste – out of London was no small task, and every step was tested with dummy materials prior to the actual removal. Temporary containment areas, air extraction and filtration systems, and special cranes were all installed to ensure there would be no contamination outside of the reactor area – even the drains were sealed to make sure nothing could accidentally escape through them. On the 1st of December, 1999, the building was handed over to the Greenwich Foundation, having been declared nuclear free, and is now used by the University of Greenwich[152].

The Royal Navy currently has ten active nuclear submarines; four *Vanguard*-class boats carrying Trident-II ballistic missiles and six 'fleet' submarines that carry torpedoes and cruise missiles. The *Vanguard* class are due to be replaced by a new *Dreadnought* class with the first, a new *HMS Dreadnought*, being built in Barrow-in-Furness. It is expected to be in service sometime in the early 2030's and the four planned boats[153] in the class are expected to cost close to 8 billion pounds each.

---

[152] To be fair to the Royal Navy (and the British Government), they were just copying the example set by the Americans. The world's first nuclear reactor was built in 1942 under Stagg Field, an old football field belonging to the University of Chicago. The population for Chicago at the time was just over three million, who had no idea that a fission reaction was going to be tested for the first time under their feet! And the first Russian nuclear reactor? This was in 1946 and was at the Kurchatov Institute in Moscow, about 10 miles from Red Square – you do have to wonder sometimes how we are all still here.

[153] The other three are to be called *HMS Valiant*, *HMS Warspite*, and *HMS King George VI*.

July 31st 1970 – An Odd Burial

Alcohol was an important part of the daily life of a sailor, going back to at least the 15th Century. Putting fresh water into barrels, then loading tons of it onto ships is great in principle, but within a couple of weeks the water starts to go brackish and undrinkable[154], and unless you make a lot of stops or capture rainwater, you will quickly find that your crew will go thirsty, eventually falling ill and dying.

To get round this, ships carried large amounts of beer. It was quite weak at less than 2%[155], but the brewing process and the alcohol meant that it would last for months rather than weeks, allowing ships to travel further before having to resupply, as well as keeping the sailors healthier (excluding alcohol-related diseases)[156]. Then the trade routes to the West Indies opened up and the Navy had access to cheap and plentiful supplies of rum.

In 1655 half a pint of rum was given to sailors, but it wasn't watered down - this was full strength at 57% alcohol or higher. One of the reasons for it being full strength was the method of storage. It needed to be kept locked up, and the safest locked places on ships tended to be the gunpowder magazines, access to which was carefully controlled. With the rum above 57%, if the barrel leaked whilst in the magazines the gunpowder would still be usable.

This led to the pursers on the ships – the warrant officers responsible for victualling the ship – to devise a test to ensure they were buying the correct strength rum. They would place a small amount of gunpowder into a bowl or in a large spoon, add a dash of rum, and then ignite it. If the gunpowder fizzled and failed to burn correctly, the purser knew they were being fobbed off with watered down rum. This led to the expression *'Gunpowder Proof'*, though I don't recommend trying this in the aisles of your local supermarket to test their stock!

By 1740, Admiral Vernon had become so exasperated with the drunkenness of sailors he ordered that the rum ration be watered down at a four-to-one ratio and served in two quarter-pint rations[157], much to the dismay of the sailors. Vernon

---

[154] Though it would still be used for cooking, being boiled in the stoves before the provisions were added (and yes, boil in the bag was not invented in the early 1970's, provisions for the men in the Age of Sail were placed into numbered mess bags and cooked in the boilers in the stoves).

[155] Fosters is 4% (in Europe), Guinness is 4.2%, and Newcastle Brown Ale is 4.7%.

[156] Depending on the area the sailors were serving in, wine could be a substitute for the beer ration, though in a lesser amount.

[157] The sailors would get a quarter of a pint at lunchtime and a quarter of a pint in the evening.

used to wear a large coat made from a material called grogram[158], and this inspired a nickname for his watered-down rum – grog.

Sailors were not allowed to share their rum ration or hoard it to give them the equivalent of a Friday night out at the pub, but they were known to surreptitiously swap some of their rum with fellow crew members in return for favours. Whether that be helping to read or write a letter home or repairing clothes, these favours could be paid for with 'sippers', a sip of your rum for a small favour, or 'gulpers', a gulp of your rum for a large favour. However, if you were caught doing this it was a punishable offence[159].

From 1795, the Royal Navy started adding lemon or lime juice and sugar to the grog to help prevent scurvy[160] and in 1824 the ration was reduced to a quarter of a pint. With the arrival of steam engines to power ships in the mid 1800's, large amounts of fresh water could be distilled from seawater so the beer ration was phased out.

In 1850, the rum ration was halved again to one-eighth of an Imperial Pint, which is 71ml, whereas a double shot from a pub nowadays is 89ml. Officers lost their rum ration entirely in 1881, and it was finally phased out for all on July 31st, 1970 – which is now known as 'Black Tot Day'.

At HMS Collingwood[161], sailors held a mock funeral and buried a bottle of rum, with a coffin, funeral procession, and pipers to mark the occasion. For those at sea when they received their final tot, some men 'buried' them at sea, whilst others wore black armbands.

One of the most famous brands of rum is Pussers, which is a corruption of the word purser. The company was formed in 1979 to produce and sell rum that was made to the blend the navy used.

---

[158] Grogram was a mix of wool and silk and was quite rough.

[159] Generally, sailors would be whipped using a cat-o-nine tails for drunkenness or other offences, and often the number of lashes would be increased if you were a repeat offender. You could receive up to 36 lashes for drunkenness.

[160] Which is why the Americans call the British 'limeys', for the limes and lime juice they carried to add to the rum.

[161] HMS Collingwood is a shore base in Fareham, England.

May 30th 1982 – HMS Invincible... Still Afloat

On April 2nd, 1982, the Falklands War[162] began when Argentinian troops invaded the *Falkland Islands*, which had been under a British flag since 1883. Prior to this, there had been French, Spanish, Argentinian, and British claims on the islands dating back to the first French settlement there in 1764.

Argentina started expressing their desire to have control of the Falklands in the mid-1950's, citing an old territorial claim, and in the 1970's the British – in particular the Foreign and Commonwealth Office – came up with a plan to transfer sovereignty to Argentina, but the islanders refused.

The claim was used by Argentinian politicians in a nationalistic way, driving public fervour and support for their parties and to win votes. When a geological survey in 1971 showed that the area around the islands had promising oil reserves, as well as the fishery rights and potential seabed mineral rights, the Falklands also had a tangible monetary value. Talks between the UK, Argentina, and the islanders continued until 1981, but no progress was made.

The initial Argentinian invasion force in 1982 came by amphibious landings, and once vehicular support arrived, they over-powered the small garrison there (68 Royal Marines, 11 naval scientists, and 23 volunteers). Once they had control of the airport, more troops were flown in, along with supporting vehicles and aircraft.

Five days later a British task force left Portsmouth with the aim of recapturing the islands. Once it had joined with other ships, there were a total of forty-three Royal Navy ships, twenty-two Royal Fleet Auxiliary ships, and over sixty merchant vessels to provide transport and logistics. This was a remarkable feat as Portsmouth Dockyard was being downsized and many workers had either just, or were just about to, receive their P45's[163].

On June 14th, the islands were liberated, but at great cost to the Royal Navy and the other armed forces. The Type 21 frigates *HMS Ardent* and *HMS Antelope* were sunk in Falkland Sound (*above*), the Type 42 destroyers *HMS Sheffield* south of the

---

[162] Called *Guerra de las Malvinas* by the Argentinians.

[163] A '*P45*' is issued when an employee leaves (or is asked to leave) his job. The equivalent in the United States would be the '*pink slip*'.

islands and *HMS Coventry* just north of Pebble Island. The Royal Fleet Auxiliary lost *Sir Galahad,* and the merchant ship *SS Atlantic Conveyor was also sunk[164].*

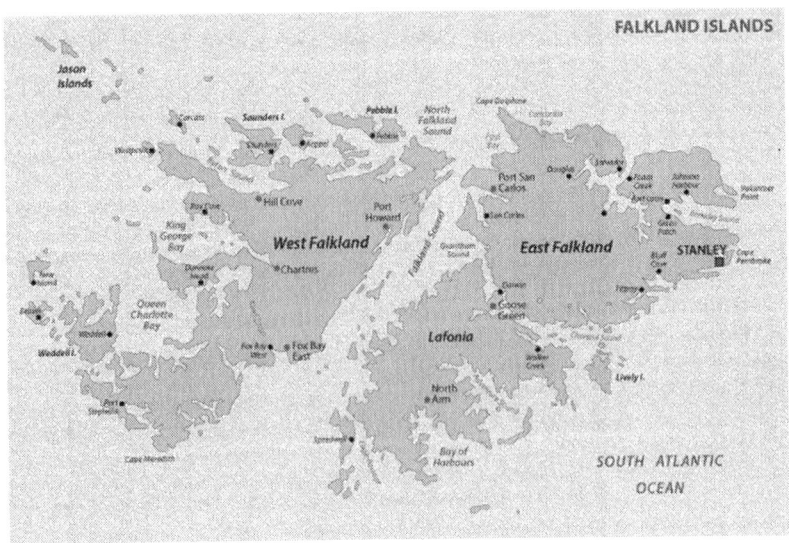

Between the 21st and 25th of May British troops began establishing a beachhead in San Carlos Water, in the north-east corner of Falkland Sound. Argentine Air Force and the Argentine Naval Aviation units heavily bombed the ships and the troops attempting to land over the five days. Despite the British shooting down over twenty aircraft, it was here that *Ardent* and *Antelope* were sunk, and *Argonaut* and *Broadsword* were damaged. *HMS Coventry* was sunk as part of this action, though she was outside of San Carlos Water, which became known as '*Bomb Alley*'.

A ceasefire was agreed, prisoners swapped, and the situation returned to its previous state, with both sides continuing to swap claims and counterclaims about the islands. In 2013, the islanders were given the opportunity to vote on their future, and 99.8% of them voted to remain an '*Overseas Territory of the United Kingdom*', though I am sure that the involved governments will drag this up again in the future.

---

[164] The loss of the *Atlantic Conveyor* badly affected the ground operations. Destroyed were three Chinook helicopters, six Wessex helicopters, and a Lynx, which should have provided fast transport for the men on the ground. Without them, the rough terrain of the Falklands had to be covered on foot. It was a forced march carrying a full load – and they covered 56 miles in three days, each carrying an 80-pound load (36 kg). The Royal Marines call this a '*yomp*' and outside the old Royal Marines Barracks in Eastney, Portsmouth, there is a statue called '*The Yomper*' which is dedicated to the Royal Marines.

Back in 1982, there was no internet and the UK was still ten years away from 24-hour news. We would get updates on the 8 o'clock news in the morning and the 6 o'clock news in the evening on the television. The information we were being given could (generally) be relied upon, though with a small amount of spin depending on the channel or the newspaper you were using. The advent of the internet means people can say or publish any *'fact'* they want, with no quality or truth-checking. One of the oddest ones to have arisen in recent years is the claim that the Royal Navy's aircraft carrier, *HMS Invincible* (RO5) was sunk during the war.

An Argentinian pilot, Ensign Gerardo Isaac, claims to have seen *Invincible* on fire on May 30th after being hit by an Exocet missile, and he had then dropped his bombs on her, resulting in her destruction. The Argentinian press even produced doctored photos showing *Invincible* on fire (the third time they had claimed the *Invincible* was sunk during the war).

How then was an intact *HMS Invincible* in Port Stanley in July, showing no signs of damage? Well, according to one of the conspiracy theorists ploughing their tripe on the internet, either: Great Britain built a replacement aircraft (in two months, when the original build took four years with another three years of sea-trials and fitting out), the Americans built one for us and shipped it to the Falklands, or the fitting out of *Ark Royal* was sped up, reducing it from four years to two months, then she pretended to be *Invincible*.

If *Invincible* had been sunk, there would also have been over a thousand deaths, more than were recorded for both sides combined, and even though there was no internet then it would not have been possible to conceal such losses. During the war, *Invincible* was held further away from the front than *HMS Hermes*[165] as she required a turbine change, which was the first time this had been done at sea. To bring her back to the UK would have meant the loss of the aircraft and flight-deck from the front-line for weeks, so the decision was made to do it in situ. Though it limited her actions whilst this was undertaken, it kept her in the right place to be useful.

So why do some people still believe *Invincible* was sunk? Patriotism? Blind trust? I can't be sure, but the people peddling this (as with many similar conspiracy theorists) get paid for the number of views they have on their YouTube channels and hits on their websites, so the more inflammatory – or appealing to public passion – they can make their content, the more money they make. If they publish

---

[165] *HMS Hermes* was a *Centaur*-class aircraft carrier, commissioned in 1959 and de-commissioned in 1984. Like the Royal Navy's latest aircraft carriers, she had a ski-ramp at the front to assist with take-offs for the jets (Harrier's back then). She was eventually sold to the Indian Navy, who used her as *INS Viraat* from 1987 until 2017.

an article on the Falklands War about the British victory that gets them one thousand views, or an article about a cover-up on *HMS Invincible* that gets one-hundred thousand views (and money), which narrative do you think they will continue to push?

24th September 1993 – The Black Flag of Monmouth

On the 24th of September 1993, *HMS Monmouth* (F235), a Type 23 frigate, was commissioned. If you managed to see her when she was active, you might have noticed two oddities, she flew a black flag next to the ensign and the name on her stern was in black paint rather than the standard red.

Nicknamed the *Black Duke*, the ship is named after the town of Monmouth in Wales, who once had a Duke. The first Duke of Monmouth, James Scott (1649 – 1685), was the eldest but illegitimate child of Charles II, and was born in the Netherlands. At the age of 13 he was given the newly created title Duke of Monmouth and was married the following month once he had reached the respectable age of 14!

He became popular with the public, especially after serving in the Anglo-Dutch Wars and the Franco Dutch War. He was a Protestant, unlike the man who would end up succeeding Charles II as James II, who was a Roman Catholic. Monmouth had the backing of many and was forced into exile in 1679 as it was feared he would try and take the throne. When his father died, he led a force back to England to try and take the throne from his uncle, the newly crowned James II.

Called the Monmouth Rebellion, it culminated in the Battle of Sedgemoor[166] on the 6th of July 1685, where the Duke – with approximately four-thousand armed men – came up against the King's army of around three thousand. It was a one-sided battle, with the King's army outflanking the rebels and only losing two-hundred soldiers in a comprehensive victory.

The Duke escaped, only to be captured two days later (*next page*), and on the 15th of July was executed at Tower Hill, London, with the executioner taking at least five blows to sever his head (*next page, courtesy of the Rijksmuseum, Amsterdam*). The title Duke of Monmouth was struck from the records, and there has never been one since, though there have been seven ships in total with the name *HMS Monmouth*.

---

[166] Sedgemoor is near Bridgewater, Somerset.

As the Duke was struck from the records in disgrace, this is why ships named *Monmouth* fly the black flag and have their names painted in black. The *Monmouth's* have battle honours including Sole Bay (1672), Barfleur (1692), Gibraltar (1704), Ushant (1747), and Camperdown (1797).

If you have a love for the 'Age of Sail', then look for the Trafalgar Times, a quarterly publication. You can find it on Amazon, Kindle, on Patreon (for PDF versions), and if you are a school you can email in to get free printed copies. Follow them on Twitter using @TrafTimes.

Appendix A – The Diamond Rock, a Poem by Henry H. Breen

Twas a morn in May, when across the bay

The Captain his spy-glass he threw;

The sun was steeping the Diamond Peak

In streams of purple and blue.

"Up! up! my lads! your anchors weigh,

We steer for the Diamond Rock:

A bolt—a bar—a shell—a spar—

We'll take her by twelve of the clock."

A voice in the ship then spake aloud:

"Beware of the Spectre, beware"—

The Captain scowl'd, the wind it howl'd,

And the Commodore 'gan to swear.

The Commodore—oh! he did lustily swear;

A thundering oath swore he :—

"I'll take the Rock by twelve of the clock,

Or the Devil he may take me!"

And out they glode, from the Royal Road,

Three frigates, a schooner, and sloop;

The Gallic Cock on the binnacle crow'd,

The pilot look'd out from the poop.

South-East the squadron shaped its course,

The red sun full in their eye:

Three days they sail'd, three nights they hail'd,

No Diamond Rock was nigh.

A voice in the prow then whisper'd low;—

"Beware of the spectre," quoth he:

The Commodore started and stood aghast;

The helmsman whistled and gazed at the mast,

And the Captain he pray'd on his knee.

"Look out, look out, go search all about;

The Diamond Rock must be here:"—

And some pull'd long and some row'd strong,

And some did steadily steer.

And all at once, as if by chance,

In the midst of the scatter'd crew,

The Diamond Rock, without shiver or shock,

Stood gallantly forth to view.

Some said 'twas a dream—some thought that the gleam

Of the moonshine their sight had enchanted;

And one there was who stoutly averr'd,

The Rock it was surely haunted.

All round the Rock the Vultures flock,

   Still round and round they go;

The sea-snakes gambol on its crest,

   And the green sharks prowl below.

And straight there issued from the Rock

   A voice that in thunder spake:

"Who hails below?—a friend or foe?"

   The French did answer make :—

"In France's name we come to claim

   This Diamond for her Crown;

If you don't yield the fortress up,

   We'll pull the fortress down."

"By conquest's right, by valour's might,

   That day thou ne'er shalt see!

By Ocean's Powers the Gem is ours,

   And ours it still shall be."

A shot, with that, laid the Commodore flat,

   Flat on the deck lay he:

The sailors raised the bleeding corpse,

   And cast it into the sea.

The fight began—from ship to ship

   The rattling balls rebound;

Through stern and hull, from shank to skull,

   Still ran the death-shot round.

And every man that falls in the van,

   Is pitch'd overboard, stiff and stark;

And every corpse in the wave that drops,

   Is swallow'd by a shark.

And up at the Fort, as if in sport,

   The foeman his cannon discharges;

The splinters of stone come down with a groan,

   And shiver his fragile barges.

And every man that falls in the Fort,

   Is cast away to the rear;

The vultures overhead pounce down on the dead,

   And bear them off to their lair.

Still round and round the sturdy Rock

   The assailants turn in vain;

They try it East, they try it West,

   No footing can they gain.

And in their wake prowl the shark and snake,

   Unsated with human gore;

While high overhead, round the English dead,

   The Vultures scream for more.

Three burning days the Sun's broad rays

   Scowl's on the scene below;

Three dreary nights the Diamond's lights
Burn'd with a lurid glow.
Three dreary nights, and on the fourth
The frigates and schooner went down—
Ah! well I ween, it cost them dear,
That Gem of the Gallic Crown.

Three burning days, and on the fourth
The Fortress' fire grew slack;
Not a creature stirred, not a sound was heard,
Save the breeze in the Union Jack.

And of the men, five score and ten,
That did the Diamond man;
Day after day, and night after night,
They perish'd one by one.

Nor less the bold besiegers—
Into the gaping surge
They dropped away, like blasted hay,
Before the tempest's scourge.

Into the gaping sea they dropp'd,
Three hundred men and more;
The gallant force sank, corse by corse,
All but the sloop and four.

Three Sailors and their Captain,
The only remnant left;

Apart from the slain they safe had lain,
Hid in the Diamond's cleft.
A death-like stillness dwelt around,
On water, earth, and air;
The Sloop and the Rock each other did mock,
With silence of despair.

And 'neath the Rock the Sloop did rock,
A blank and bootless wreck;
And over the Sloop the Rock did stoop,
A barren Ocean-speck

And now forth issuing from the cleft,
Like spectres from the tomb,
The Captain and his comrades three
The steep embrasure clomb.

The ramparts past, around they cast
Their eyes, some foe to find:
The quick and the dead alike had fled,
Nor left a trace behind.

No trace to show what dauntless foe
Their squadron so fiercely had batter'd;
Save a ragged flag that frown'd from the crag,
With blood and brains bespatter'd.

And over the wall the flag they haul,
And hoist the Tricolor;

Then away! away! across the bay
They hie to the mainland-shore.
And lo! from the wave, as if from his grave,
A gallant Tar uprose;
The flag Tricolor in shreds he tore,
And flung it at the foes.

The Captain and his comrades three
Turn'd up their dazzled eye;
And there instead of Blue-White-Red,
The English Cross they spie.

"A ghost! a ghost!" the Captain cried:
And bent his trembling knee;
"A ghost I a ghost! O Christ! we're lost!' —
Exclaim the seamen three.

But ere they could run, the Ghost with his gun
He slew the seamen three:
The Captain alone sent forth a deep groan,
Which show'd unslain was he.

Then, seizing a spar, he rush'd at the Tar,
And fell'd him to the earth;
The Tar with a bound sprang up from the ground,
And grasp'd him by the girth.

With clash and din around they spin;
The Diamond's edge they near:
And over the steep down into the deep
They plunge, and disappear!

A death-like stillness dwelt around,
On water, earth, and air;
The Sloop and the Rock each other did mock
With the silence of despair.

And 'neath the Rock the Sloop did rock,
A blank and bootless wreck;
And over the Sloop the Rock did stoop,
A barren Ocean-speck!

The award-winning Mariner's Mirror Podcast is the world's no.1 podcast dedicated to all of maritime and naval history. Presented by Dr Sam Willis the podcast has been downloaded and viewed by millions, worldwide. With regular interviews and constant innovative video content the Mariner's Mirror podcast will change the way that you think about the world's maritime past. It is published in association with the Society for Nautical Research and the Lloyd's Register Foundation.

Further Resources

The Society for Nautical Research

https://snr.org.uk/

Founded in 1910, the Society was instrumental in saving HMS Victory, and the founding of the National museum's at Greenwich and Portsmouth. They cover all aspects of maritime history, not just the Age of Sail, and should be one of your go-to clubs.

History Hit

www.historyhit.com

History Hit is a subscription video and podcast channel filled with short to medium length documentaries about historical subjects. They cover everything, not just nautical matters.

The Nautical Archaeology Society

www.nauticalarchaeologysociety.org

The NAS have three core strands: Education, Research, and Publication, and they run a variety of courses for all levels. Note that you do not have to be a diver to join or benefit from this group, courses include shoreline recording and object preservation and recording techniques

The Naval Dockyards Society

https://navaldockyards.org/

The NDS guides and produces research on naval dockyards around the world and their associated activities, including shipbuilding, ordnance, victualling, medicine, construction, history, and preservation.

The Navy Records Society

www.navyrecords.org.uk

The Navy Records Society was created to publish original material on the history of the Royal Navy. They publish regular volumes every year and cover all aspects of the Royal Navy.

The 1805 Club

www.1805club.org

The 1805 club focusses on the navies of the world between 1714-1837, not just Trafalgar, and have an extensive research and educational program. With excellent regular publications and events (pandemics allowing), they have a good presence worldwide.

The Nelson Society

https://nelson-society.com/

All things Nelson, of course.

The Trafalgar Way

https://www.thetrafalgarway.org/

Created to commemorate the 271-mile route from Falmouth to London taken by Lieutenant Lapenotiere to bring the news of the Battle of Trafalgar (and the loss of Nelson) to the Admiralty. This site has a huge amount of information relevant to the time and some excellent teaching resources.

National Historic Ships

www.nationalhistoricships.org.uk

A searchable register of the over 1,800 historic ships fleet in the UK

If you are thinking of visiting Portsmouth Historic Dockyard to see the Mary Rose, HMS Victory, the National Museum of the Royal Navy, and the other sights there, then consider 'Exploring Portsmouth Dockyard' – not only is it a guide to the historic buildings and memorials you can see there, it also tells you how to get the most out of your visit to this site (two days to see everything), as well as other hints and tips.

Index

12th Submarine Flotillas, 60

13th Submarine Flotillas, 60

4th Battalion, 59

617 Squadron, 80, 81

Acre, bombardment of, 41

Admiral Graf Spee, 71

Admiral of the Fleet, 23

Admiralty and Marine Affairs Office, 12

Aids to Scouting, 45

aircraft carrier, 82

Aitken, James, 16

Akko. See Acre, bombardment of

Alberta, 82

alcohol, 85

Altmark, 71, 72

Ance Au Loup, 40

Argentine Air Force, 88

Argentine Naval Aviation, 88

Armistice, 65

arson, 16

Arzew, 75

Atlantic Conveyor, 88

Baden-Powell, Robert, 45

Bailey and Pegg, 45

Baldwin, John, 18

Barbary macaques, 76

Barolong tribe, 45

Battle

of Bita Paka, 74

of Jutland, 60, 65

of Lake Erie, 38

of Sedgemoor, 90

of the Nile, 79

of the River Plate, 72

of Trafalgar, 23, 27, 32, 33, 34

Beatty. Vice-Admiral Richard, 60

Bedlam. See Bethlem Hospital

beer, 85

Beijing, 69

Belgian Congo, 49

Bethlem Hospital, 15

Bethlem Royal Hospital, 15

Bingham, Arthur, 37

Bismarck, 80

Black Duke, 90

black flag, 90

Black Tot Day, 86

boat race, 28

Bogart, Humphrey, 52

Bomb Alley, 88

Bomber Command, 82

Bonaparte, Napoleon, 31

Bonchurch, 10

Boulogne, 9

Boxer Rebellion, 69

Breen, Henry H., 32, 93

Bristol, 17

British Pathé, 35

Brownsea Island, 45

Buller, Redvers, 47

bumboats, 21

Cadiz, 32, 33

Calais, 57

callaloo, 30

Cape Town, 50

Capet, Hugh, 8

Capitaine Mehl, 57

careening, 19

Carew, Gawen, 9

Carew, George, 9

Carr, Josephine, 13

Carron Company, 31

carronade, 31

Castle

Calshot, 9

Hirst, 9

Southsea, 9

cat-o-nine tails, 86

Certificate of Protection, 36

Chamberlain

Neville, 47

Chaney, Benjamin, 68

Chatham, 27, 38, 39, 57

Chichester Shoals, 26

Churchill, Winston, 47, 73, 77

Clerk Comptroller, 11

Clerk of the King's Ships, 11

Coastal Command, 82

Commonwealth, 65

Congressional Gold Medal, 38

conspiracy theory, 89

Continental Marines, 24

copper, 19

copper-bottomed, 19

court martial, 22, 41

Cox, Ernest, 68

Culdrose, Royal Naval Air Station, 48

cutlass, 69

Dam Busters, 80

Dardanelles, 54

dazzle, 53

Deane, Charles, 22

Deane, John, 22

Devonport, 27

Distinguished Service Cross, 56

Distinguished Service Medal, 56

dog, 68

Dover Straits, 56

Duguay-Trouin, 34

Duke

of Monmouth, 90

of Normandy, 8

Dunnose, 26

Earl St. Vincent, 23

Eddystone lighthouse, 12

Edersee dam, 78

El-Shazliya Mosque, 41

England Expects..., 33

Eshelby, Thomas, 24

Falkirk, 31

Falkland Sound, 87, 88

Falknor, Jonathan, 26

Falmouth, 35

Field of the Cloth of Gold, 8

First Lord of the Admiralty, 47, 73

floating out, 20

Foreign and Commonwealth Office (FCO), 87

Forester, C.S., 52

Fort

Blockhouse, 18

Edward, 28

Saint Louis, 28

Fort Royal, 28

Fort-de-France, 28

Fremantle, Thomas, 24

Friedrich der Grosse, 67

Furse, Dame Katharine, 13

Fyssher, Robert, 11

gallows, 16

geodetic, 78

George Cross, 55

German East Africa, 49

German High Seas Fleet, 60, 65

Gibraltar, 21, 76

Gibson, Guy, 80

Girl Guides, 45

Godley, Alexander, 77

Graf von Götzen, 49

Grand Fleet, the, 83

Grand Military Tournament and Assault-at-Arms, 46

Gravina, Frederico, 32

Gray, James, 15

Great Dane, 68

Great Game, the, 43

Great Harry, 7

Great Lakes, the, 38

Great Western Steamship Company, 42
Greenwich, 84
Greenwich Foundation, 84
grog, 86
grogham, 86
Guerra de las Malvinas, 87
Gunpowder Proof, 85
Harwich, 65
Hedwig von Wissman,, 49
Henry Grace à Dieu, 7
His Majesty's Marine Forces, 23
HMAS
  Australia, 61
HMAS *Australia*, 63
HMS
  Alecto, 42
  Antelope, 87, 88
  Ardent, 87, 88
  Arethusa, 16
  Argonaut, 88
  Ark Royal, 89
  Association, 12
  Brilliant, 13, 58
  Broadsword, 88
  C1, 58
  C3, 58
  Centaur, 28
  Colibri, 38
  Collingwood, 48, 86
  Comet, 41
  Cossack, 72
  Courageous, 61
  Coventry, 88
  Culloden, 23, 25
  Curieux, 29
  Defiance, 14
  Diamond, 31
  Dreadnought, 42, 83, 84
  E11, 54
  Eagle, 13
  Edgar, 43
  Emerald, 23
  Exeter, 71
  Fame, 70
  Fearless, 62, 63
  Fifi, 51
  Forte, 47
  Gladiator, 26
  Gorgon, 39
  Goshawk, 38
  Grampus, 56
  Guerriere, 36
  Hermes, 89
  Hood, 25
  Implacable, 34
  Impregnable, 26, 27
  Intrepid, 58
  Invincible, 89, 90

Iphigenia, 58
Ithuriel, 61
K11, 61
K12, 61
K14, 61
K17, 61
K22, 61
K3, 62
K4, 62
K6, 62
K7, 62
King George VI, 84
Litchfield Prize, 13
Little Belt, 37
M33, 53
Mary, 12
Monmouth, 90
Mortar-Bomb, 13
Newcastle, 13
Niger, 50
Northumberland, 12
Nubian, 56
Pine, 75
Pique, 39, 41
Porcupine, 75
Pork, 75
Powerful, 43
Prompte, 38
Psyche, 38
Queen Elizabeth, 43, 82
Rattler, 42
Reserve, 13
Resolution, 13
Restoration, 12
Royal George, 20, 22
Seahorse, 24
Sheffield, 87
Sirius, 58
Stirling Castle, 12
Temeraire, 83
Terpsichore, 23
Terrible, 43, 46
Theseus, 23, 24
Thetis, 58
Tonnant, 14
Valiant, 83, 84
Vanguard, 12, 82
Vesuvius, 13
Victory, 14, 19, 20, 21, 27, 34, 37
Vindictive, 58
Warspite, 22, 84
Whiting, 70
Wilton, 81
York, 13
Zealous, 23, 25
Zubian, 58
Zulu, 57
Honourable Artillery Company the Duke of York and Albany's

Maritime Regiment of Foot, 23
Hood, Samuel, 25, 28, 30
Hornblower, Horatio, 52
Howe, Richard, 21
hulks, 27
ice-cream, 83
impressment, 35
in ordinary, 35
Indian Navy, 89
Infantería de Marina, 23
INS
  Viraat, 89
Isle of Wight, 9, 10, 20, 26, 40
Israel, 41
Jack the Painter, 16
Jenkins, Michael, 26
Jervis, John, 23
John the Painter, 16
Jones, Captain Edward Pitcairn, 47
Jøssingfjord, 72
K-class submarines, 61
Keeper of the King's Ports and Galleys, 11
Keeper of the Storehouses, 11
Kempenfelt, Richard, 22
Kerr, John Graham, 53
King
  Æthelstan, 8
  Charles I, 18
  Charles II, 90
  Clovis I, 8
  Edward the Confessor, 8
  Francis I of France, 8
  Harold, 8
  Henry V, 18
  Henry VII, 7
  Henry VIII, 7, 11
  James II, 90
  William I, 8
King, Ernest, 83
King's Majesty Council of his Marine, 11
King's Ships, 7
Kingani, 49
Kingdom of England, 8
Klaver Camp, 69
Kretschmer, Otto, 75
Kurchatov Institute, 84
Labrador, Canada, 39
Ladysmith, 46
Lake Erie, 38
Lake Ontario, 38
Lake Tanganyika, 49
Lancaster bomber, 78
Langsdorff, Hans, 72
larboard, 21

101

Last Post, 69
Le Curieux, 28
Lee, John R., 49
Liemba, 52
Lieutenant of the Admiralty, 11
limeys, 86
Lisbon, 26
Lord High Admiral, 12
Lord Nelson, 45
Lützow, 71
Mafeking, 44, 45
Mafikeng. See Mafeking
Malta, 55
Maritime Warfare School, 48
Martinique, 28, 30
Mary Rose, 7, 9, 20, 22
Master of Naval Ordnance, 11
May Island, 62
Mediterranean, 77
Mentions in Dispatches, 59
militia, 11
Mimi, 50
Möhne dam, 78
Montevideo, 72
Moscow, 84
Mountbatten, Francis, 83
mutiny, 17
Nant-y-Gro dam, 79
Nasmith, Martin, 54
National Museum of the Royal Navy, 74
Navy Board, 11
Nelson, Horatio, 23, 25, 27, 32, 33, 45
New Principle of Gunnery, 79
Nisbet, Fanny, 25
Nisbet, Josiah, 25
Nore, the, 17
nuclear reactor, 83, 84
Nuisance, Just, 68
Odiham, 17
Officer-in-Charge of the Apes, 77
Old Royal Naval College, 84
Operation
    Catechism, 81
    Chastise, 80
    Torch, 75
Orde, John, 23
Orkney Islands, 65, 83
Ostend, 58
Ottoman empire, 43
Overseas Territory of the United Kingdom, 88
paddle wheels, 41
Paris Peace Conference, 66
Parliament heel, 20

Pasco, John, 34
Pasley, Charles, 22
pay, 17
Pepworth Hill, 46
Perry, Oliver Hazard, 38
Perutz, Max Ferdinand, 82
Plymouth, 17, 35
Popham's Telegraphic Dictionary, 34
Port Stanley, 89
Portsmouth, 9, 10, 20, 26, 27, 35, 39, 40, 75, 87
Portsmouth dockyard, 41
Portsmouth Harbour, 18, 22
Portsmouth Point, 21
press gang, 35
Prien, Günther, 75
promotion, 23
propellor, 42
purser, 85
Pussers Rum, 86
Pyke, Geoffrey, 82
Pykrete, 82
Q-ships, 53
Queen
    Anne, 12
Queen Elizabeth class aircraft carriers, 81
Quota System, 36
R100 airship, 78
RAF
    Marham, 81
    Scampton, 80
Red Admiral butterfly, 33
Relief of Ladysmith, 44
reviews, 5
Reynolds, Robert Carthew, 28
RFA
    Sir Galahad, 88
Richelieu, Cardinal, 23
River Hai, 70
River Medway, 27
RMS Leinster, 13
Robert the Magnificent, 8
Robins, Benjamin, 79
Rodgers, Commodore John, 36
Rolls-Royce, 83
ropery, 17
Rossiya, 43
Rosyth, 83
Rous, Captain Henry John, 39
Royal Australian Air Force, 81
Royal Australian Navy, 74
Royal Fleet Auxiliary, 87
Royal Marines, 23, 28, 59, 88

Royal Navy, 12
Royal Norwegian Navy, 72
Royal Tournament, 48
Rubbing salt into the wounds, 29
Rurik, 43
Russia, 43
San Carlos Water, 88
Sandown, 10, 11
Santa Cruz, 23, 25
Scapa Flow, 60, 65
Scott, James, 90
Scott, Percy, 46
Scouts, the, 45
scurvy, 30
Sea of Marmara, 54
Seaford, 11
Seiner Majestät Schiff, 65
Shakespeare William, 11
Short Brothers, Belfast, 52
Siege of Mafeking, 45
Simon's Town, 68, 69
sippers, 86
sloop, 42
SM UC-1, 57
SMS Seydlitz, 65
snorkel, 54
Society of Righteous and Harmonious Fists, 69
Solent, 20
Solent, the, 9
Sorpe dam, 78
South Africa, 68
Southampton, 10
Spalding, Charles, 22
Spice Island, 21
Spicer-Simson, Lieutenant-Commander Geoffrey, 50
Spithead, 17, 20, 21
squadrons, 23
SS Archimedes, 42
SS Great Britain., 42
St. Helen's Roads, 9, 40
St. Helens, 10
Strait of Belle Isle, 39
Strickland, Thomas, 39
Studding sails, 40
STVOL, 81
Surveyor and Rigger of the Navy, 11
Taku forts, 70
Tallboy Bombs, 80
Tenerife, 23
Teredo Navalis, 19
The African Queen, 52
The Battle of the River Plate, 72
The Dam Busters, 80
The Greatest Raid, 58

Tirpitz, 80
Topp, Erich, 75
Toulon, 31
Tournament of Shadows, the, 43
Toutou, 50
Tower Hill, 90
Tower of London, 76
Treasurer of Marine Causes, 11
Treaty of Utrecht, 76
Tribal-class, 56
Trinity nuclear test, 68
Tromsø Fjord, 80
Troubridge, Thomas, 25
Type 23 frigate, 90
U-12, 50
U-29, 83
U-602, 75
UB-123, 13
U-boat, 65, 75, 82
United Services Institute, 68
United States, 35

United States Marines Corps, 24
University of Greenwich, 84
Upkeep bomb, 79
USS
    Constitution, 37, 78
    President, 36
    Spitfire, 36
Vernon, Edward, 85
Vian, Philip, 73
Vickers Wellington, 78
Victoria Cross, 55, 59
Vikings, 8
Villeneuve, Pierre-Charles, 32
von Reuter, Ludwig, 66
War
    American Revolutionary, 16
    Anglo-Dutch, 90
    Crimean, 43
    Egyptian-Ottoman, 41
    Falklands, 87
    First Gulf, 13

Franco-Dutch, 90
Great, 65
Habsburg-Valois, 8
Italian, 8
of 1812, 38
of the Spanish Succession, 76
Second Boer, 49
Second Boer, 44, 45
Warrant Officers, 14
West Indies, 30, 85
White, George, 46
Wilkinson, Norman, 53
Williams, Thomas, 22
Women's Royal Navy Service, 13
World War I, 13, 49, 56, 74
World War II, 35, 68, 75, 76, 78, 81
Wren, Sir Christopher, 84
Wrens, 13
Yihéquán, 69
yomp, 88
Yomper, the, 88
Zeebrugge, 58

I am working on a second volume of *Navy Bites* as there are so many stories waiting to be told. Volume II should be out in January 2024. *AJN*

Take a tour through the iconic ship that is arguably Portsmouth's most famous landmark, *HMS Victory*.

This book guides you deck-by-deck through the ship, bringing to life the wooden walls and the lives of the sailors who were on her.

Written by local author and guide AJ Noon, for every copy sold a donation is made to the National Museum of the Royal Navy, who look after the ship.

The Essential
Visual HMS Victory
AJ Noon

Printed in Great Britain
by Amazon